John S. Wilson

JAZZ:

The Transition Years
1940–1960

APPLETON-CENTURY-CROFTS

DIVISION OF MEREDITH PUBLISHING COMPANY, New York

PRINTED IN THE UNITED STATES OF AMERICA

Contents

Illustrations

Foreword

There was a time before World War II when the jazz world was small and comfortably intimate. It was a world that followed familiar, traditional patterns.

Big bands were continuing to steer a course charted many years before by the band leader, Fletcher Henderson, and his arranger, Don Redman. Small groups were still holding to formulas that dated back even farther.

The jazz fancier was a member of a minority group that was sprinkled helter-skelter around the globe, a minority group so minor and isolated that belonging to it sometimes had overtones of membership in a secret society.

Then—seemingly without warning—this little world burst apart. Jazz exploded internally as its form and content changed beyond recognition. It exploded externally, flooding out into the welcoming lap of a worldwide public. The music spread in all directions at once. It moved toward strange and distant horizons at the same time that its neglected past was being rediscovered. Jazz became educational, cultural, respectable and fashionable. It penetrated every layer of American society and created unbounded confusion among both its old adherents and its newly found supporters.

The story of jazz up to World War II has been told and retold from a variety of viewpoints. But most jazz histories cover the war years and the immediate postwar years hurriedly and briefly, leaving the years since then in limbo.

The purpose of this book is to fill in some of the details of these missing years—the two explosive decades of jazz history between 1940 and 1960. It is assumed that the reader has some familiarity with the development of jazz during the earlier decades of this century (this period is covered unusually well in *The Story of Jazz* by Marshall Stearns). Jazz since 1960 is still too close to be viewed in perspective but a knowledge of the events of the two preceding decades can help to provide an understanding of why jazz in the sixties is what it is.

Jazz: The Transition Years

ONE

The Stage Is Set

The end of World War II was, as novelist Ralph Ellison has noted, "an exceptional moment and the world was swinging with change."

In jazz, the change seemed to occur with shattering suddenness.

Actually, the fuse that set off this change had been lit almost a decade earlier. In the middle of the 1930's, Count Basie's band came east from Kansas City with Lester Young playing oddly beautiful, floating saxophone lines while Jo Jones slyly broke up the expected steady drumbeat with strange and provocative accents. In Teddy Hill's band in Harlem, drummer Kenny Clarke was moving in the same direction while Hill's twenty-year-old trumpet player, Dizzy Gillespie, began to search restlessly beyond the guiding influence of Roy Eldridge. Out in Oklahoma, Charlie Christian, stirred by contact with Lester Young, was transferring Young's linear style to the guitar, and in Kansas City Charlie Parker, who had also been affected by Young, was beginning to find his potent musical personality.

Near New Iberia, Louisiana, Bunk Johnson, an old New Orleans cornetist, had been discovered working in a rice field and some students of archaic jazz were wondering whether he still might be able to play. In jam sessions at the Big Bear Tavern near San Francisco, trumpeter Lu Watters was rousing the interest of some local musicians in the forgotten jazz of New Orleans.

These were some of the sparks that were to kindle the greatest upheaval that jazz had ever experienced.

But in the late thirties the swing era was in full flower and the popular furor that accompanied it completely obscured the likelihood that anyone would notice these sparks flying among the tinder. Only Lester Young was sufficiently prominent to be noticed and, while it was conceded that he was changing the jazz conception of the tenor saxophone, it didn't seem likely that he might be changing all of jazz.

A world swept up in war early in the forties could give little attention to relatively obscure activities on the subterranean levels of jazz. Service in the armed forces removed jazz fans of all degrees from contact with the music for three, four or five years. Moreover, a ban on recording, imposed by the American Federation of Musicians on its members while the union attempted to negotiate new contract terms with the record companies, lasted from mid-1942 until late in 1943. This ban eliminated the principal means for the dissemination of new jazz ideas at what turned out to be a vital period in the music's development.

One result of this combination of events was that, when rational civilian life returned, jazz fans in general knew little or nothing about the things that had taken place in jazz during the preceding years. As they tried to piece together the old familiar elements of their prewar lives, they tended to assign to jazz the characteristics that they had known before—the characteristics which, in fact, defined jazz in their eyes.

But when they attempted to reassemble the pieces they

identified as jazz, they no longer fell into place properly. It was a disconcerting discovery. Orrin Keepnews, a man with prewar jazz roots who subsequently has produced distinctly postwar jazz records, remembers his first exposure to the new developments when he returned from service in the Pacific in 1945. It was a jarring experience.

"A very bright-eyed young man whom I had just met insisted on playing some new records for me," Keepnews recalled. "He gave the impression of being about to produce the Holy Grail, or at the very least a live rabbit out of an old top hat. But all I could hear was a screeching exhibitionistic trumpet, a whining saxophone, very little discernible melody, and no sort of reliable beat. I hated it and informed the young man in a patiently paternal way (I was at least three years older than he) that this noisy fad could never take the place of The Real Thing."

It was the isolation in which The Real Thing had given way to the Noisy Fad and in which other changes in jazz had taken place during the war years that made it seem as though an explosion had occurred in the mid-forties.

Suddenly there was something called bop.

Suddenly there was a high-powered revival of early traditional jazz.

Suddenly the familiar big bands were being sidetracked by small groups.

Suddenly jazz was a concert music, no longer a music for dancing.

Suddenly there were Australian jazz bands, of all things, playing jazz in Czechoslovakia, of all places.

At least, it seemed sudden. Actually, the transition was quite gradual. To some who were able to keep abreast of developments, it even seemed cumbersomely slow.

The stage was being set for the change as the decade of

3

the thirties came to an end. That was a period when jazz was dominated by the big bands that had begun to enter jazz in the middle twenties, spearheaded by the bands of Fletcher Henderson and Duke Ellington. So important had the big band become in jazz by the 1930's that even Louis Armstrong, who had reached a peak in the twenties with a series of recordings made with small groups (his Hot Five and Hot Seven), gave up this successful setting late in 1929 to play in front of big bands. He continued to work with a frequently uninspiring succession of big bands until they were blown out from under him by the jazz explosion of the mid-forties.

The end of the thirties was the swing era, a remarkable period when Benny Goodman's band gave popular dance music a strong jazz orientation and so captured the public's fancy that it succeeded to (and even exceeded) the acclaim that had previously been accorded the "sweet" music of Guy Lombardo and Wayne King. The attraction of the swing band was so complete that it blanketed jazz with suffocating thoroughness. There was no longer sufficient audience to sustain the small jazz bands through which the music had been developing for three decades. Jelly Roll Morton, a major figure of the twenties whose orchestral conception of jazz did not fit in with the swing band formula, was sunk in obscurity through most of the thirties. Red Nichols, whose brisk and stylish Five Pennies had brightened the twenties, tried to conform to the demands of the thirties by organizing a big band but it was a dismal comedown from his earlier small groups. Dixieland survived in the thirties mainly through the efforts of Bob Crosby's Bob Cats, a small group that was nestled safely within Crosby's successful big band.

The state of small group jazz in the thirties is summed

4

up in the brief career of Muggsy Spanier's Ragtime Band. When it was formed in 1939, Spanier's seven-piece band was considered the best small jazz band to appear since Armstrong's recording groups of the late twenties. Yet it had to break up in a matter of months because, except for a couple of night clubs in New York and Chicago, there was no place where a group of this type could work. Everything was oriented toward the big band (and within a year, Spanier was leading one).

Among the big bands there were varying degrees of jazz depth. Many of them—Duke Ellington's, Jimmie Lunceford's, Earl Hines'—were thoroughgoing jazz bands that had preceded the coming of the swing bands. Others were essentially the traditional sweet bands that kept up with the times by acquiring a thin jazz veneer.

As the veneer grew thinner through constant repetition, public sympathy toward the jazz elements in swing wore thin. By the end of the thirties the time was ripe for the return to ascendancy of the primarily sweet dance band. It was signaled by the rise of Glenn Miller's orchestra, which reversed the proportions of hot and sweet elements that Goodman had popularized. Where Goodman's had been a hot band with a sweet side, Miller's was a sweet band with some hot aspects.

As the remaining swing bands became increasingly formula-ridden, it seemed to many jazz followers that their music was reaching a dead end in 1940. First, the big swing bands had succeeded in eliminating most small jazz groups. Now, the swing bands themselves seemed to have run their course. Even such topnotch bands as Count Basie's and Jimmie Lunceford's appeared to be heading downhill. Practically the only bright spot in the drab surface that jazz presented in 1940 was provided by the indomitable Duke

Ellington who was leading what was considered then (and can still be considered in the perspective of a quarter of a century) the finest band he ever led.

But that was just the surface. The world was swinging with change and, under the deceptive surface, changes were already bubbling in jazz.

TWO

Revolution

Four musicians are customarily identified as the main bridges leading from swing to the new jazz that became known as bop—Lester Young, Roy Eldridge, Jimmy Blanton and Charlie Christian. They were all transitional figures but their individual relationships to the changes that occurred in jazz were markedly different.

Roy Eldridge, a trumpeter, provided the narrowest bridge of the four. Coming in the wake of Louis Armstrong, he chopped up the flowing, often stately lines with which Armstrong built his solos, developing in their place a bristling, biting style that created a sense of agitated excitement. This was the style that first attracted Dizzy Gillespie and it was on Eldridge's variation of Armstrong that Gillespie built his own personal manner which established the trumpet hallmarks of bop. Eldridge, who is the only one of the four transitional musicians still living, has made no attempt to follow Gillespie's lead but has preferred to polish and hone his own way of playing. By doing this, he has retained his individuality (strengthened it, in fact) and has escaped the kind of finger-pointing to which changing fashions can subject a jazz musician, for, while Eldridge is not actually "modern" in his concept, neither can he be pigeonholed as old-fashioned.

Jimmy Blanton's contribution was decidedly more far-reaching. He was a bassist from St. Louis, Missouri. Duke Ellington heard Blanton there in 1939, when he was only eighteen, and immediately took him into his band. Blanton brought a new conception of the string bass to jazz. Traditionally it had been used to produce a steady stream of quarter notes, mostly as a supplementary force in the rhythm section or occasionally in short solos. But Blanton had such facility on this normally cumbersome instrument that he was able to take melodic and harmonic approaches on it that had not been attempted before. Instead of bumbling along in the background, Blanton's bass became as fluid a part of the ensemble as the trumpets, saxophones or trombones.

"Blanton found the bass a thumper," Barry Ulanov wrote, "and left it a jumper."

The impact of Blanton's virtuosity on the use of the bass in jazz can be judged not so much from the fact that he influenced the playing of every jazz bassist who followed him (although this in itself is an impressive achievement) but by the remarkably short time in which he was able to make his influence felt. Blanton was heard with Ellington for less than two years when his career was cut short by tuberculosis. He was only twenty when he had to stop playing and he died a year later.

By a remarkable coincidence, Charlie Christian's situation duplicates Blanton's almost exactly. Like Blanton, he was a trans-Mississippian Midwesterner (from Oklahoma City, Oklahoma). He also took the shackles off an instrument in the jazz rhythm section (the guitar) and had a lasting influence on its use. He was hired by Benny Good-

8

man in the same year that Blanton joined Ellington; tuberculosis forced him to stop playing at the same time that it brought Blanton down; and when he died within months of Blanton, Christian was just a year older than the bassist.

Christian, however, did not find new resources in an established jazz instrument, as Blanton did. Instead, he introduced a new instrument, the electric guitar, and a method of playing it that effectively threw its predecessor, the unamplified guitar, into the discard. The unamplified guitar had been used in jazz primarily as a rhythm instrument, occasionally as a somewhat timid and hard-to-hear solo instrument playing either chorded or single-string passages. A few attempts had been made to use electric guitars before Christian's arrival—notably by Eddie Durham of Count Basie's band and by Floyd Smith with Andy Kirk—but they seemed to be little more than twangy novelties. Nonetheless, it was hearing Durham playing his electric guitar with Basie in 1937 that stimulated Christian, then a pianist, to get a guitar.

"I never in my life heard a guy learn to play guitar faster than he did," Durham commented later.

Working with bands through the territory north of Oklahoma City, Christian learned to use the guitar as though it were a horn, creating long, flowing, looping lines instead of the staccato chopping that had always been customary among guitarists. He was able to do this because notes could be sustained on an amplified guitar as they could not be on the regular instrument. And with amplification, the sound of the guitar could be raised to a point where it held its own with other instruments. Thus, not only could it take a comfortably heard solo role, but it could also become a third melodic line in an ensemble, instead of being relegated to the rhythm section.

9

When Christian came to New York with Goodman in 1939, his method of playing seemed less remarkable than the instrument he used. The structure of his playing—the rhythmic accents and the flow of his phrases—followed lines that had already been made familiar by Lester Young with Count Basie's band. Christian had frequently heard Young when their paths crossed in the Dakotas or in Oklahoma City and there is little doubt that Young made a profound impression on the young pianist-guitarist. In New York, Christian quickly found a congenial group of musicians playing at Minton's Playhouse in Harlem. He felt so much at home there that he bought an extra amplifier and kept it at Minton's so that he could always drop in when he had finished his night's work with Goodman without carrying his regular amplifier uptown.

It was at Minton's and at Clark Monroe's Uptown House that a group of nonconformist musicians stimulated each other to evolve the new jazz ideas that became bop. Christian was in on the early stages of this stimulation—was, in fact, one of the prime stimulators—but he did not live long enough to see bop take shape. By 1941 his playing days were over and he was in a tuberculosis sanitarium on Staten Island where he died the following year.

"If Charlie had lived," said Kenny Clarke, a drummer who was one of the major contributors to the new movement, "he would have been a real modern."

So far as actual contact with the core of musicians who developed bop was concerned, Christian was a more active part of the movement than any of the other transitional men. Blanton and Young sat in frequently at these sessions but Christian was a regular only to the extent that his touring with Benny Goodman permitted. Yet it was Young, essentially a loner, an isolated man who spent most of his life within a thick protective shell, who was the most important of the four in carving out the path that led from swing and the culmination of one period of jazz to the new jazz of the forties. Young's contribution was not just the brief but vital encounter of a Blanton reorienting the string bass or Christian validating the electric guitar. What he had to offer was a continuation of a process that has been a source of development in jazz since its earliest days—the reworking in personal terms of something that has already been established and investing it with so much individuality that it seems entirely new. Young's approach appeared so individual—even, to some, perverse—that it was years before it was accepted, much less viewed as a guide to the future.

In the late twenties and early thirties when Young was developing, the accepted style for a tenor saxophonist was that of Coleman Hawkins—dark and gutty in tone, played in heavy, chopped, charging phrases. Young's light, airy, flowing, relatively unaccented lines were almost the direct antithesis of this, a contrast that reached a classic climax when Fletcher Henderson hired Young to replace Hawkins, who had gone to Europe, and Young found that he was resented by the other men in the band because he sounded so unlike Hawkins.

"Finally I left and went to Kansas City," Young once recalled. "I had in my mind what I wanted to play and I was going to play that way."

The way that Lester Young wanted to play was based on the fluidity and relaxation of the old New Orleans jazz-men. Over this he mixed a light, lyrical sound derived from that of the C melody saxophone played by Frankie Trumbauer in the Jean Goldkette and Paul Whiteman bands and a technique influenced by Bud Freeman's tight, whirligig style on tenor saxophone. Thus equipped, he created solos that often seemed, in the apt description of Whitney Balliett, "a collection of evasive, pleasantly melodic hums that had the muted, introverted quality of a sound-proofed room and that seemed to end before they had even been stated."

The purity of his sound was a shocking change from the visceral tone of the established Hawkins school and his avoidance of vibrato contrasted sharply with the lusty throbbings of the Hawkinsites. And as if this were not enough, his rhythmic accents and the varied lengths of his phrases ran counter to accepted fashion.

All of this accounted for his slowness in finding a wide audience. But even in the days before he began to achieve acceptance with the Count Basie band in the late thirties, his influence was being felt. Out in the stretches of the Dakotas, he had impressed young Charlie Christian. In Kansas City, Missouri, the then obscure Charlie Parker was said to know every note that Young played. And by 1939, when Coleman Hawkins came home from a long stay in Europe, he learned that Lester Young had suddenly found his audience and had become the dominant influence on tenor saxophone.

Primarily through such slightly younger musicians as Christian and Parker, Young played an essential part in establishing the setting in which bop developed. Yet the strongest reflection of Lester Young's musical personality was not left on bop but on the reaction that followed bop —cool jazz. Young himself, however, was not really a part of the cool movement when it arrived late in the 1940's any more than he had been a real part of the bop movement. He was always indomitably himself, going his own slightly offbeat way. He seemed most at home not in any of the modern jazz areas to which he opened the doors but in the relaxed, swinging company of the pre-bop Kansas City-bred musicians who were around him in the late thirties.

The real revolutionaries of jazz were the men who gained some sense of direction from Young, from Christian, from Blanton, from Eldridge and from still others such as Jo Jones, the drummer in Basie's band. Jones broke away from the accepted custom among big band drummers of hitting out each of the four beats in a measure with the foot pedal on his bass drum. He shifted his steady four-beat activity to the cymbal, backed up by similarly steady beats from bass and guitar, so that his bass drum could be used more fluidly as an accent or prod to alter or accent the rhythmic direction of a soloist. The possibilities for the use of complex polyrhythms that this opened up, and which became one of the characteristics of bop, were also explored by Kenny Clarke, the drummer in Teddy Hill's band in the late thirties when Dizzy Gillespie was in Hill's trumpet section. Clarke added to the complexity of the rhythmic attack by playing patterns on the snare drum with his left hand while his right carried the beat on the top cymbal.

The unrest that bubbled beneath the conformist surface of the big bands in the swing era was fed by after hours sessions that could be found almost every night in Harlem as the thirties came to a close. They took place at the Kentucky Club, at Puss Johnson's and at Clark Monroe's Uptown House, but by late 1940 these sessions were concentrated in a backroom in Minton's Playhouse, a bar and cabaret on West 118th Street next to the Cecil Hotel. When Teddy Hill, who had broken up his band in 1939, became manager of Minton's in 1941, he brought Clarke in as leader of the house band, a group that included Thelonious Monk on piano. Monk was already such an individualist in his ideas of harmony that, as Mary Lou Williams has recalled, "there were few musicians who could run changes with him" when he first arrived at Minton's.

Hill allowed the musicians to play whatever they wanted. The resultant stimulation of the searching and seeking carried on by Monk, by Clarke and such regular sitters-in as Charlie Christian and Dizzy Gillespie, who was then with Cab Calloway's band, made Minton's a focal point for musicians. "They used to come from miles around," Clarke has recalled, "from Chicago, from everywhere to hear us play."

And not only to listen but to sit in. Some of the sitters-in became a problem. "There were always some cats showing up there who couldn't blow at all but would take six or seven choruses to prove it," Gillespie complained. Both Gillespie and Clarke are agreed that the first formalization of what had been until then individual and disorganized experimentation came about as part of an effort to discourage the undesirable sitters-in.

"On afternoons before a session," Gillespie explained, "Thelonious Monk and I began to work out some complex variations on chords and the like and we used them at night to scare away the no-talent guys. After a while we got more and more interested in what we were doing as music and, as we began to explore more and more, our music evolved."

The music, at that time uncategorized and unnamed, was marked by complexities of harmony and rhythm that were new to jazz and by the elimination of stated melodies, leaving only the chord progressions—the skeleton on which a melody is constructed—as the basis for the soloist's improvisations.

Both as explorer and organizer, Dizzy Gillespie was a key figure in establishing the outlines of this music. He took his first tentative steps toward it by trying to move away from Roy Eldridge's shadow while he was in Teddy Hill's band in 1937. Later, when he was playing in Edgar Hayes' band in 1938, Gillespie found a passage in a Rudy Powell arrangement that struck him as interesting and different.

"It really got me," he recalls. "I played it over and over and realized how much more there could be in music than what everybody was playing. There was a lot there that nobody had been getting."

The next year, when he joined Cab Calloway, Gillespie kept working on his new harmonic ideas despite Calloway's denunciation of them as "Chinese music." During intermissions at the Cotton Club, Calloway's bassist, Milt Hinton, would go up on the roof to practice with Gillespie as he tried different chords and progressions.

"There were things he attempted to do that he couldn't," Hinton has said. "He didn't wholly make everything he tried but he got to me and I admired him for what he tried. Like he would try a long-range progression with a high note at the end and he missed it. Cab would get very angry. Some of the guys in the band would say, 'Nice try, kid; try it again.' But most of them didn't think he had anything or would amount to anything."

The most vitalizing force in the new music was a musician who was not a part of the *avant-garde* clique that first gathered at Minton's. Charlie Parker had drifted in and out of New York from Kansas City a few times before 1941 without making contact with the musicians who were evolving the new ideas, although Gillespie, Clarke and Monk heard him in 1940 when he played briefly at Monroe's Uptown House. Their interest in him then, however, was the fact that they thought he sounded like Lester

Young although Parker played alto saxophone instead of Young's tenor. Parker did not join in the Minton sessions until 1942 but by that time he had developed some discoveries of his own.

The basic revelation came to Parker, by his own account, in a chili house on Seventh Avenue in Harlem. He was jamming there in December, 1939, with a guitarist named Biddy Fleet. At the time, Parker had become bored by the stereotyped changes that were customarily played. "I kept thinking there's bound to be something else," he once recollected. "I could hear it sometimes but I couldn't play it."

As he worked over *Cherokee* with Fleet, Parker suddenly found that by using higher intervals of a chord as a melody line and backing them with appropriately related changes, he could play this thing he had been "hearing." For the next three years he worked on this discovery. Much of this time he spent with Jay McShann's band and, just as Gillespie had worked on his ideas within the framework of the arrangements being played by Edgar Hayes and Cab Calloway, Parker used his new approach in his solos with McShann, although he apparently encountered less animosity than Gillespie.

Despite his search for the "something else" that he could only hear before he figured out how to play it, Parker was essentially a jazz traditionalist. That is, his customary material was the most basic element in jazz—the blues. What he did with the blues, however, was definitely something else. He expressed himself through a kaleidoscope of surprises, mixing long and short melodic lines, simple rhythms and complex ones, legato with staccato, full-bodied tone with thin shrillness. His rhythmic accents sometimes fell on the beats as expected, at other times between beats, creating, as Max Harrison has pointed out, "the effect of two streams of rhythm" through the opposition of on-and-off beat accentuations. At the same time, both he and Gillespie refused to be hemmed in by the usual construction of a melody, cutting through bar-lines and other divisions of a tune with streams of notes that might break off just as unexpectedly as they had been launched. It was an attack that often had a shattering effect on musicians encountering it for the first time. Dave Tough, one of the few swing era musicians who made the adjustment to the new music, remembered with awe his first hearing of the Dizzy Gillespie-Oscar Pettiford group on Fifty-second Street in 1944.

"As we walked in," Tough reported, "these cats snatched up their horns and blew. One would stop all of a sudden and another would start for no reason at all. We never could tell when a chorus was supposed to begin or end. Then they quit all at once and walked off the stand. It scared us."

Before bop was to reach Fifty-second Street in 1944, however, it still had some seasoning to go through. By 1943 a new incubator had taken shape—the Earl Hines band which had gone through an infusion of new personnel late in 1942 under the guidance of Billy Eckstine, who sang with the band, and of Budd Johnson, a tenor saxophonist who had been Hines' right-hand man for seven years. The band included Gillespie and Little Benny Harris, another trumpeter who was an ardent follower of Gillespie and Parker. When Johnson left early in 1943, Parker came in, switching from alto to tenor to take the job. The second pianist and girl singer in this band was Sarah Vaughan.

This Hines band is destined to go down in jazz history surrounded by almost as much mystery as has grown up

17

around the prowess of the earliest of all jazz heroes, Buddy Bolden, and for precisely the same reason—there is no recorded evidence of its work. During the brief year of its existence, the American Federation of Musicians imposed a ban on recording. By the time the ban was lifted late in 1943, the band had spent months straggling through a tour of Army camps at steadily diminishing salaries and the key men had dropped out.

However, it provided the inspiration for the first big band that had the temerity to base its musical policy on the new music. This band was formed by Eckstine in 1944 with Gillespie as musical director, a saxophone section that included Parker, Gene Ammons and Lucky Thompson, and with Sarah Vaughan and Eckstine as the vocalists. The band quickly found that an appreciation of bop was still limited.

"Out West nobody liked us," said Parker. "In the Middle West the Negroes liked us. But in New York everybody loved us."

In the same year, the new music moved downtown from Harlem to New York's Fifty-second Street. Early in 1944 Gillespie and Oscar Pettiford, a bassist who had followed the trail blazed by Jimmy Blanton, took a quintet into the Onyx Club. This was the first organized bop group. During the next two years The Street, a term which identified the block between Fifth Avenue and Sixth Avenue on Fifty-second Street, attracted more and more followers of the new style musicians. By 1945 a major white band, Woody Herman's, had become affected by the new approach and, pairing it with a tremendously dynamic presentation, became the dominant big band in jazz.

As interest in the new music—known usually as re-bop or be-bop—spread, animosities flared between older musicians and adherents of the new forms. Louis Armstrong, a prime target of the polemicists of the new school who disdained Armstrong's followers as "moldy figs," lashed out at the taunts of the "boppers" with an anguished wail.

"They want to carve everyone because they're so full of malice," he protested. "All they want to do is show you up and any old way will do as long as it's different from the way you played before. So you get all them weird chords which don't mean nothing and first people get curious about it just because it's new but soon they get tired of it because it's really no good and you got no melody to remember and no beat to dance to. So they're all poor again and nobody is working and that's what the modern malice done for you."

Gil Fuller, who wrote fast, complicated arrangements with such titles as *Things to Come* for a big band organized by Gillespie in 1946, took an opposing view.

"Modern life is fast and complicated," Fuller said, "and modern music should be fast and complicated. We're tired of that old New Orleans beat-beat, I-got-the-blues pap."

"I can't stand it," declared Eddie Condon in expounding the "fig" view of bop. "I can't understand it and I can't see how those guys who play it can either. That type of music—that weird, try-to-figure-it-out serenade-to-a-toilet-in-mid-ocean stuff seems to me as musical as tonsilitis."

The new musical gods quickly acquired an infallibility that could not be questioned in front of their supporters. Early in 1946 a man who had been reporting on jazz for several years was approached by an eighteen-year-old in a Fifty-second Street club called the Spotlite.

"You like Teddy Wilson, don't you?" the youngster declared.

The writer admitted that he did, that Wilson—a polished, precise pianist who became popular during the swing period—was very good.

"Dizzy doesn't think so," proclaimed the eighteen-year-old.

"Well," shrugged the writer, "Dizzy's only one man."

His opponent's eyes suddenly blazed.

"Look, Jack," he growled. "Dizzy knows, see!"

One of the few reasoned expressions that could be heard came from Duke Ellington who, being neither a moldy fig nor a bopper, was above the battle.

"Why be surprised that be-bop is ridiculed?" he asked. "Jazz and swing got the same treatment in their early days, too. Anything that's alive must progress and music is alive. There are young minds, wonderful minds working on fresh musical ideas. These ideas have spread and some part of them will be incorporated into the music of tomorrow."

Time, of course, softened most of these adamant attitudes and a few years later Bobby Hackett, a member in good standing of the traditionalist school, could exclaim with a twinkle, "The other night I started to think I was sounding like Miles Davis and I liked it."

And Davis himself, dismayed at the smug superficiality of many of the young, untried musicians who proclaimed themselves as boppers sprung full-blown from the head of Charlie Parker, dampened their habitual dismissal of the past.

"I don't like to hear someone put down Dixieland," Davis declared. "Those people who say there's no music but bop are just stupid. It just shows how much they don't know. I never played Dixieland myself. When I was growing up I played like Roy Eldridge, Harry James, Freddie Webster and anyone else I admired. You've got to start way back before you can play bop. You've got to have a foundation."

One thing that most of the young recruits to the bop revolution had in common was no foundation. Plenty of intense, burning, one-track desire they had, but no foundation. They laboriously learned all the most familiar flights created by Parker or Gillespie and religiously played them over and over throughout their attempts at solos.

When Charlie Parker died in 1955, pianist Lennie Tristano said that if Parker had wanted to invoke plagiarism laws, "he could sue almost everybody who's made a record in the last ten years."

Actually, the mere ability to play these runs was something of an accomplishment when one considers that these were often relatively untrained instrumentalists.

But the flood of fumbling imitators that were attracted to bop—and by the latter forties scarcely any young musicians would consider anything else—created an additional handicap for the new music in its efforts to communicate to a wide public, adding the element of stereotypes of varying degrees of aptitude to the seeming strangeness of the music even when it was skillfully played.

Those listeners who had had difficulty finding the melody when it was strained through a swing or Dixieland band were now totally lost. In many cases the tunes that were used by the boppers were the same old familiar ones that had served their purposes in early phases of jazz—*Indiana, Cherokee, Just You Just Me, I Got Rhythm, Stompin' at the Savoy,* among others. But they were changed far beyond casual recognition. Completely new melodies were built on the chord progressions of these favorite tunes that were so far removed from the originals that they were given new titles and new copyrights. Leonard Feather, a veritable Pooh-Bah of jazz who, among his many other roles, enjoys being a "tune detective," has found *Just You Just Me* lurking beneath tunes called *Evidence, Spotlite,*

Mad Be-Bop and *Ray's Groove; Indiana* disguised as *Donna Lee, Ice Freezes Red, Trumpet at Tempo* and *Tiny's Con; Cherokee* as *Blue Serge, Dial-Ogue* and *Ko-Ko;* and *How High the Moon* as *Bean at the Met, Bird Lore, Hopscotch, Indiana Winter, Low Ceiling, Ornithology* and *Slightly Dizzy.*

In 1946 Parker and Gillespie ventured to the West Coast with four colleagues to reveal their new music to the previously uninitiated California outlanders. To say that their engagement at Billy Berg's in Hollywood was a failure would be a gross understatement. It was not simply that they were not appreciated. Their music was actively hated on every side. Berg didn't like it. The patrons at Berg's couldn't stand it.

"Man, they used to stare at us so tough," Gillespie declared afterwards. "They thought we were just playing ugly on purpose."

They did not even find sympathy among the musicians in the band with which they shared Berg's bandstand, Slim Gaillard's group, a situation that finally led to fisticuffs. A Los Angeles radio station became so aroused by the music that it banned bop from the air—at least, from its share of the air. *Time* magazine, suddenly discovering this music that had been played almost within earshot of its home office in New York for a couple of years, advised its readers that "what bebop amounts to is hot jazz overheated, with overdone lyrics full of bawdiness, references to narcotics and doubletalk." A few years later *Time* topped this classic of misinformation by doing a cover story on modern jazz without mentioning Charlie Parker.

The only aspect of bop that had real appeal to the public was its decor—the beret, dark, heavy-rimmed glasses and goatee that were publicized as the standard bop garb. Bop kits, consisting of a real beret, empty glasses frames and false goatees, enjoyed a brisk sale. (More than a decade later the same equipment was being peddled around San Francisco as a "Beatnik Kit.")

The primary salesman of this aspect of bop was Gillespie, an uninhibited and practical man who, as a trumpet player, found it more comfortable not to shave his lower lip; who chose a beret as his headgear because it was the only kind of hat he could put in his pocket and, therefore, would not lose; who wore glasses to see properly and, in choosing heavy rims in the mid-forties, merely anticipated the popular taste of his countrymen by several years. His association with these hallmarks of the bopper reaped him vast personal publicity, much of it of dubious value. In the end, all that this sideshow approach succeeded in doing was to make bop seem ridiculous and to detract from Gillespie's efforts to present bop as a valid musical form.

By 1949 the general public was still putting up a strong resistance to bop and even the jazz audience was wearying of repeated servings of what had become clichés. Gillespie by then had reached a point of desperation in his attempts to develop an audience for the big band he was leading.

"Bop is part of jazz and jazz is music to dance to," he told a *Down Beat* reporter. "The trouble with bop as it's played now is that people can't dance to it. They're not particular whether you're playing a flatted fifth or a ruptured 129th as long as they can dance."

But by then the dancing audience had been lost to jazz and within a year Gillespie had no band, no recording contract and no plans for the future. Bop, he declared, had come to the end of the road and the fault, he said, lay with the boppers themselves.

"Like the guys that would come into my band," he explained, "they seem to have a different state of mind from guys going into other bands. They don't think about showing. They think it would be a drag if people were to think they like what they're doing. They think it's enough if they just blow. If you want to make a living at music, you've got to sell it."

To a degree, Gillespie was right. The initial, groundbreaking phase of bop had indeed reached the end of its road. But looking back at this period from the vantage point of 1955, Woody Herman could appraise this as a very important era for jazz.

"It wouldn't have had the impact that it did otherwise," he said. "In the last five years the good has been cultivated and what we have left today is whatever was valuable in it all.

"The funny and sad thing is that today you can play the same music that was damned in 1947 and 1948 and get away with it completely. I suppose that there are at least two reasons for this: First, that sheer repetition many times sells a product and, second, that the music is really more settled today with much more emphasis on driving swing than bop generally had."

THREE

Reaction

The steady linking of action and reaction that has been one of the essential aspects of the growth of jazz was working overtime during the 1940's. The twists and turns of jazz became more violent than they had ever been before. First came the complete switch in direction evolved by the men who developed bop, a switch urged on them by their boredom with the rut into which jazz had fallen. Then, after the bop men had established a fiery, frenetic norm for their music, reaction once again set in. This time the swing of the pendulum went back beyond the frenzy of bop, beyond the outgoing emotionalism of the swing bands of the thirties, to a withdrawn, understated manner that subsequently became identified as "cool jazz."

Like all jazz labels, "cool jazz" was applied after the fact and, as usual, there was considerable disagreement about the precise area that it should cover or, in fact, if it existed at all. Miles Davis, a trumpeter, is frequently cited as the epitome of the cool style because of the cleanly shaved, vibratoless tone and the deliberate, carefully stated nature of his playing in the late forties and early fifties when the cool reaction was taking place. Subsequently, however, Davis developed a style that was distinctly hot and emotional (while retaining and polishing some aspects of his early cool style) and the musicians he employed in his group in the late fifties were as far from the cool element as one could imagine. Gerry Mulligan, who is also counted in the cool school more by association than on the basis of performing style, has attributed the basic cool approach primarily to pianist Lennie Tristano rather than to Davis. And Lee Konitz, an alto saxophonist and disciple of Tristano who is considered the prime cool exemplar on his instrument, has taken the view that the cool approach is descended from the playing of Louis Armstrong with his Hot Five in the middle twenties—a style that most jazz followers would consider the epitome of hot jazz.

In one notable respect, the progenitors of cool jazz differed radically from the men who had raised the bop revolution. It was one of the distinguishing factors of bop that it turned its back on the past of jazz. The slate was wiped clean and a fresh start was being made. Necessarily, the pioneering boppers such as Gillespie and Parker had musical roots in this past which they could not disown. Nor did they want to disown them. These roots were the platform, the foundation on which they could build, but the new structure they created obscured that foundation completely. Many of their followers, however, being unaware of the foundation, seeing only the structure, were inclined to assume that jazz began with bop so that they not only ignored the past of jazz but were ignorant of it.

This was not true of those whose probing and investigations produced cool jazz. Lee Konitz, as has been noted, was very much aware of Louis Armstrong, even if his interpretation of Armstrong's playing might seem strange to some listeners. Stan Getz, who holds a position on tenor saxophone equivalent to Konitz's on alto, played in Jack Teagarden's band when he was just a teen-ager and developed a great admiration for the veteran trombonist.

"I've never heard any modern trombone player get the sound Jack Teagarden gets," Getz once said.

Mulligan, who was growing up at a time when most youngsters his age were convinced that the jazz world began and ended with Charlie Parker, was listening not only to Parker but to Bob Crosby's big Dixieland band, to Jimmie Lunceford's orchestra and, like Getz, to Jack Teagarden.

"Teagarden has always been my big idol," Mulligan has declared. "He has everything a great jazz musician needs to have: a beautiful sound, a wonderful melodic sense, a deep feeling, a swinging beat and the ability to make everything—even the most difficult things—sound relaxed and easy."

At a time when it was assumed that no modern jazz musician could mention Dixieland without spitting, Miles Davis announced that he did not like to hear anyone put down Dixieland.

"Those people who say there's no music but bop are just stupid," he said. "It just shows how much they don't know. You've got to start way back there before you can play bop. You've got to have a foundation."

Recognition of this need for a foundation meant that the proponents of cool jazz were exploring consolidators rather than the pragmatic experimentalists that the early bop musicians had been. Gil Evans, an arranger whose influence pervaded the early cool efforts, had a foundation that was probably broader and more deep-rooted than that of any other musician active in the emergent postwar jazz. Evans once listed for Nat Hentoff, in a *Down Beat* interview, some of his early jazz interests—"the sound of Louis' horn; the people in Red Nichols' units like Jack Teagarden and Benny Goodman; Duke's band; the McKinney Cotton Pickers; Don Redman. . . . I was also interested in popular bands, like the Casa Loma approach to ballads."

Evans, a pianist, was a Canadian who developed in the dance band milieu of the thirties and forties. He led his own band in California for five years during the 1930's and when Skinnay Ennis, the "breathless" singer and drummer in Hal Kemp's band, took over Evans' band in 1939 Evans remained with it as an arranger. Another of Ennis' arrangers was Claude Thornhill, a pianist who had been prominent in the New York jazz world earlier in the thirties and who had helped to launch the New York career of singer Maxine Sullivan with his arrangement for her of *Loch Lomond*. Thornhill formed a band of his own shortly after Ennis took over the Evans band and a year or so later Evans shifted his arranging allegiance from Ennis to Thornhill.

Thornhill by then had begun to evolve the sound that was to be characteristic of his orchestra all through the forties—a still, hanging sound founded on a vibratoless use of horns. Evans had always been intrigued by sounds per se. He told Hentoff that, as a boy, he could tell what kind of car was coming down the street with his back turned. Sound was one of the aspects of music that interested him most and he was fascinated by Thornhill's distinctive use of sound.

When Evans went to work for Thornhill, the band was working toward a sound that approximated that of French horns through a blending of trombones and woodwinds and by having the trumpets and trombones play into derbies. In 1941 Thornhill went all the way and brought French horns into his band, a move that caused the general register of the band's playing to be lowered to accord with the range of the French horns, giving the calm, pastoral sound that Thornhill was working toward an even more somber effect.

Later, in the mid-forties, Thornhill extended the somber depth of his band's sound even further by adding a tuba, an instrument that had once been the common bass instrument in jazz groups but had rarely been used since the late 1920's. Instead of using the tuba simply as an accent in the rhythm section, Thornhill wove it into the ensemble harmonic pattern of the band as a whole.

By then, several jazz musicians had moved through the Thornhill band—Irving Fazola, the brilliant New Orleans clarinetist; Danny Polo, a clarinetist and tenor saxophonist who spent most of his career in Europe and England where he was featured with Ambrose's orchestra; Red Rodney, one of the more personal bop trumpeters; and young Lee Konitz. John Graas, who was one of the pioneering jazz performers on French horn in the fifties, was an early Thornhill horn man. In the late forties, Gerry Mulligan was contributing arrangements to the band and Evans was feeding it arrangements of Charlie Parker tunes—*Yardbird Suite, Donna Lee* and *Anthropology.*

A coterie of young jazz musicians developed around Evans, searching, footloose youngsters who met in Evans' one-room apartment in New York. It was on Fifty-fifth Street, three blocks north of what was then the heart of the jazz world, Fifty-second Street. To get to it—as Dave Lambert, the singer, who lived in the apartment for a while with his wife and daughter and several other musicians, has remembered—"you had to go down a short flight of stairs, pass a Chinese laundry, through a boiler room, and there it was—home."

There, listening to records and talking, Evans, Mulligan,

Davis, pianist John Lewis and arrangers such as John Benson Brooks, Johnny Carisi and George Russell felt their way toward new approaches to jazz. Much of their attention focused on the sound of the Thornhill band. Evans and Thornhill, despite their mutual interest in the development of this sound, eventually separated in their feelings of how it should be used. Evans felt that the sound itself could sustain interest for only a limited time, that there had to be mobility within the context of the sound. Thornhill, on the other hand, appeared to be aiming for an almost stationary effect with the heavy sonorities of the group hanging suspended in the air while his piano trickled limpidly through them.

"If he could have had his way," Evans said, "I think he would have had the band hold a chord for a hundred bars with him compensating ably for the static effect with the activity of his piano."

The disparity in their viewpoints had become so basic by 1948 that Evans left the band. The Thornhill sound, he said, had become so bleak that it sometimes had a hypnotic effect.

"The band could put you to sleep," he complained.

But the pervading influence of the overall Thornhill sound was reflected that same year when Miles Davis organized a nine-piece band to carry out some of the talk that had gone on in Evans' apartment. One of their objectives was to expand the limited form to which ensemble playing had been reduced by the bop musicians whose performances consisted almost entirely of solos sandwiched between unison passages. The Thornhill-Evans sound struck them as a viable vehicle for the kind of ensembles that interested them.

As a result, Davis built his group as a miniature of the

Thornhill band. It included French horn and tuba along with trumpet, trombone, alto and baritone saxophones, piano, bass and drums—the smallest number of instruments, as Evans pointed out, that could get the sound and still express all the harmonies that the Thornhill band used. Arrangements were contributed by Evans, Mulligan and Carisi and the group got a two-week booking at the Royal Roost, a club on Broadway just above Times Square where impresario Monte Kay and disc jockey Symphony Sid Torin had instituted the first modern jazz policy in New York. To emphasize its policy, the Roost advertised itself as "The Metropolitan Bopera House." Later the "nonet" got an engagement at the Clique, another club farther north on Broadway, which subsequently became Birdland. That might well have been the end of the group because it made no records at that time.

But the reason that it was not recorded was that another recording ban had been imposed by the American Federation of Musicians. This ban blacked out recording activities through almost all of 1948. Recording companies meanwhile had their eyes and ears alerted for groups that they would like to record when the ban was ended. Davis' nonet caught the attention of Capitol Records and shortly after the ban was lifted in mid-December, 1948, the Davis group was reassembled in a recording studio for the first of three sessions that were to stretch out over a period of fourteen months.

The records that came out of these sessions—*Boplicity, Israel,* the very Thornhillian *Moon Dreams,* among others—were to have a profound effect on the development of jazz in the fifties although their initial impact was slight. They influenced the basic concept of what was to be identified as "West Coast Jazz." They provided musicians with the

31

thought-provoking foundation from which much of the "chamber jazz" of the fifties grew. And the group itself included several musicians who were to be potent guides in the jazz developments that lay ahead—John Lewis, Gerry Mulligan, Gunther Schuller, Lee Konitz and Max Roach, not to mention Davis himself and, of course, arranger Gil Evans.

For Davis, these recordings and his work with the group represented his emergence from an oddly tentative period in his career. He had come to New York from East St. Louis, Illinois, in 1945, ostensibly to study music at the Juilliard School. But he was soon swept up in the bop activity on Fifty-second Street. For a while he lived with Charlie Parker. He prowled the clubs at night, writing down on match covers some of the chords that he heard, and spent his days at Juilliard practicing these chords instead of going to classes. He finally quit the school when, as he said, "I realized that I wasn't going to get in any symphony orchestra. And I had to go down to the Street at night to play with Bird [Parker] or Coleman Hawkins, so I decided to go that way—all the way."

Davis at that time was struggling to follow the pattern being set by the bop men although his natural inclinations and his own capabilities ran in a different direction. He had been guided away from playing with vibrato by one of his early teachers in St. Louis. It was better to learn to play without vibrato, this teacher advised him, because "you're going to get old and start shaking anyway."

Later, when he got to New York, Davis was disturbed by his inability to play high, fast passages, like Dizzy Gillespie.

"It's because you don't hear up there," Gillespie explained to him. "You hear in the middle register."

Although he was plagued by technical shortcomings, Davis in the middle forties was part of an inner core of bop men who got many recording dates. Aware of his own deficiencies, Davis was sometimes so stricken by the work of the musicians around him that he could not play. (Gillespie, playing piano at one recording session, was forced to double on trumpet when Davis froze.)

"I used to quit every night," Davis has said, referring to this period. "The tempo was so up. The challenge was so great."

An English critic, Michael James, has noted the very slow progress that Davis made during these years.

"The same faults are found on all his recorded solos," James pointed out. "A small range that seems to embarrass his invention, a tendency to fluff notes at faster tempo, and a tone which too often borders upon the platitudinous."

With the formation of his nonet, Davis appeared to have found his proper métier, one in which he was not limited by lack of technique and which more properly expressed his personal musical feelings. Once this step had been taken, Davis went on, somewhat slowly at first, to become one of the major jazz personalities of the fifties, a musician with a style so strongly individual that he was at first copied widely, and later, as his influence became pervasive, putting the more thoughtful trumpeters in the position of consciously avoiding his characteristics lest they lose their own individuality.

The recordings made by the Miles Davis nonet have subsequently been reissued on a twelve-inch LP titled *Birth of the Cool* and it has become widely accepted that they represent the origin of cool jazz. It would be more correct to call them *an* origin of the cool, for similar influences were at work at the same time in other places.

33

While Gil Evans' apartment was serving as the scene for the discussions that led to the formation of the Davis nonet, a band was playing at Pontrelli's, a Spanish ballroom in Los Angeles, that had a saxophone section made up of four tenor saxophonists who were all musical descendants of Lester Young—Zoot Sims, Herb Steward, Jimmy Giuffre and Stan Getz. Playing arrangements by Giuffre and Gene Roland, the four tenors achieved a blend that was far lighter and purer than might have been expected from such a combination. Woody Herman, who had broken up his tremendously successful First Herd late in 1946 to settle in California for a while, reorganized his band in 1947 and hired the saxophonists at Pontrelli's almost en masse. He incorporated Sims, Steward and Getz in his band (they were joined in the saxophone section by Sam Marowitz and Serge Chaloff) and he bought from Giuffre an arrangement using the voicing that the four saxophonists had developed, *Four Brothers.*

Four Brothers set the tone for this Second Herman Herd of 1947–1949 and, primarily through Getz, moved it in a "cool" direction that reached its peak in *Early Autumn,* a ballad developed by Ralph Burns from the final section of *Summer Sequence,* a long work he had written for the Herman band in 1946. Of the four saxophonists, Getz was the one most deeply influenced by the coolness in Young's playing. (Sims, coming from the same source, placed his emphasis on Young's swinging drive to such an extent that his characteristic style became essentially "hot.")

The derivation of Getz's coolness from Young takes us in a direct line to what may very well be considered the roots of cool jazz. Young's sound was a very conscious attempt to produce on a tenor saxophone the kind of clear, limpid sound that Frank Trumbauer had gotten from his C

34

Melody saxophone in the twenties. Trumbauer, in retrospect, can be seen to be a distant forerunner of the cool
school and so, in some respects, was his constant colleague
in those days, Bix Beiderbecke. Aside from the overt evidences of what might be considered cool characteristics in
Beiderbecke's cornet playing, the path that leads from
his work to the period when cool jazz emerged as a dominant form can be traced through Bobby Hackett, whose
style is deeply rooted in Beiderbecke's and who was, in
turn, one of the favorites of the music teacher in St. Louis
who gave Miles Davis' style a formative shove when he
urged Davis to avoid vibrato.

Under the impetus of success with *Early Autumn,* Getz's
playing became more and more feathery. His surfaces were
honed down to a smooth, boneless slither that, like the
Thornhill sound, often seemed to hang suspended in the
air. By 1950, Michael James has noted, Getz's tone was
"purified to such an extent that it takes on from time to
time the quality of a whisper. The general construction of
a solo is intensely disciplined. . . . The beat has been
divested of all emphasis: with the systematic elimination
of all obvious rhythmic highlights, the ultimate effect is
one of polite but nonetheless insistent swing."

This was a far cry from the lusty, gut-driven swagger
with which Coleman Hawkins had produced the first
vitally distinctive jazz style on the tenor saxophone. It was
even a good distance from the looping, lifting swing with
which Lester Young had propelled his solos. Young, as
Michael James has pointed out, was concerned with the
highly personal presentation of a tune, a presentation in
which the tune was never absolutely transcended. With
Getz, on the other hand, the general approach was un-
compromisingly expressionistic so that the tune functioned

35

merely as a vehicle and had no intrinsic value of its own.

Getz's approach suited the tenors of the time and by the end of the forties his influence had spread among young tenor men much as Young's had ten years earlier and Hawkins' a decade before that.

A similar thing was happening in the stylistic development of the alto saxophone, although in this case the circumstances were somewhat different. The most persuasive influence on this instrument, Charlie Parker, was still at the peak of his playing power. What's more, he had arrived as an influence only relatively recently. Consequently the Parker influence was not displaced by the cool manner of Lee Konitz, who was the leading exponent of the style on alto. But the mere fact that Konitz could have any influence at all in the face of Parker's towering presence is significant.

Konitz represented still another contributing factor to the creation of the cool sound of jazz in the late forties. He had been associated with the Evans-Davis explorations both as a member of the Thornhill band and as a participant in the recording sessions by Davis' nonet.

But the primary conditioning source on Konitz was Lennie Tristano, a blind pianist who, in the late forties, drew around himself a small school of followers, including Konitz, who remained all through the fifties a part of—and almost all of—the Tristano school. Tristano has been singled out by Bill Russo, a trombonist, arranger and teacher, as the first jazz teacher.

"For the first time in jazz's history," Russo declared, "we have a man who modified the procedure of the past, evolved new ideas of operation, and was able successfully to communicate them."

Unlike others in jazz who have tried to make use of

sources outside jazz, Tristano applied none of the specific techniques of non-jazz art music, according to Russo.

"He has applied the basic intellectual presuppositions of the great composers, with whom he is on familiar terms, without using their exact methods. In other words, he has applied his mind to music, observing how this process took place earlier, and yet forming a music exclusively based on basic jazz materials."

In describing his music, Tristano has said, "Our harmonies are strongly impressionistic. Melodically, I've tried to go beyond bop which adheres largely to the given harmonic structure; we don't restrict ourselves to the chord when we play melody. Our rhythms are superimposed one on the other. Sometimes I play three different rhythms at once, while the other boys are each playing separate ones."

The music played by the Tristano sextet came out in long, billowing, unshaded lines that frequently flowed through and around each other in a manner that was at once drivingly propulsive and matter-of-factly stated. In a study of Tristano, Harvey Pekar has remarked on the "special emotional climate" that resulted.

"There is emotion in his work," Pekar said, "but it is different from any other kind of emotion I've heard in jazz. It is a cool climate, like that of Lester Young . . . but unlike Young, Tristano has no blue tinge at all in his work. And where Young is relaxed and amused, Tristano is reserved and austere."

Konitz, in the middle forties, found in Tristano's musical ideas a sense of purpose that he had been missing before. Tristano, Konitz said, "laid out a direction for me." Previously his primary influences had been Charlie Parker and Lester Young.

"I always knew I wanted to be a musician," Konitz ex-

37

plained. "I didn't know what kind of a musician I'd be. I enjoyed improvising but I didn't know much about what to do—until I met Lennie."

Under Tristano's guidance Konitz developed a light, pure-toned, unemotional style that quickly gave him a reputation as the coldest of the newer jazz musicians of the late forties. His playing set the style for other Tristano saxophonists, notably Warne Marsh and Ted Brown, both tenor saxophonists, and could be heard to some extent in the work of such alto men as Paul Desmond, Art Pepper and Lennie Niehaus. But Konitz's influence was less evident in the United States than it was overseas. When Marshall Brown traveled through Europe in the late fifties screening candidates for the International Youth Band that played at the Newport Jazz Festival, he remarked on the fact that "the alto players, almost without exception, were influenced by Lee Konitz."

In this country the cool influence was felt most strongly away from New York where much of the basis for it had originated. Aside from the Konitz influence in Europe, the primary evidence of a "cool school" was the development of what became identified as "West Coast Jazz." One of the prime movers in establishing the foundation of this school was a man who was not closely associated with the cool elements in New York—Shorty Rogers, a trumpet player. Rogers had been a sideman and arranger in Woody Herman's band but he was identified mainly with the First Herman Herd, a tremendously hard swinging group, rather than the Second Herd which housed the *Four Brothers* voicing, although he played in both. Subsequently, he was one of the trumpets that gave Stan Kenton's band much of its brassy bellicosity.

When Rogers left the Kenton band in 1950, jazz had,

38

during the preceding thirty years, made some sporadically notable appearances on the West Coast. It was there in 1922 that the first jazz recording by a Negro band—a group led by trombonist Kid Ory—was made. It was there, in Venice, California, in the middle twenties that Ben Pollack organized the band that was to include among its members at one time or another most of the great white jazz musicians of the ensuing decade. It was there in 1935—at the Palomar Ballroom in Los Angeles—that Benny Goodman's orchestra finally found its audience after more than a year of failure. It was there—at the Philharmonic Auditorium in Los Angeles in 1944—that Norman Granz launched the Jazz at the Philharmonic series that was to have an overwhelming influence on the manner in which jazz was presented. And in the forties, for the first time, a successful big jazz band was launched and centered on the Coast—Stan Kenton's.

In 1948 Howard Rumsey, a bassist who had spent most of the decade playing with Kenton, started a series of Sunday jam sessions at the Lighthouse, a club at Hermosa Beach, south of Los Angeles. Although the California penchant for jazz at that time seemed entirely oriented toward Dixieland—Charlie Parker and Dizzy Gillespie had had their unnerving engagement at Billy Berg's only two years before—Rumsey's Lighthouse sessions caught on and soon were doing so well that jazz was put into the club on a full-week basis. When Shorty Rogers moved out of the Kenton ménage, he moved in with Rumsey's group at the Lighthouse which then included Jimmy Giuffre, the saxophonist who wrote *Four Brothers*. At the same time the records made by Miles Davis' nonet in New York were getting into circulation.

Rogers began writing arrangements that made use of the

basic sound of the Davis group and the voicing ideas of Giuffre along with a swinging attack that stemmed from Count Basie's band and climactic concepts that had their roots in the styles of both the Herman and Kenton bands. The result was a somewhat more emotional form of cool jazz than was being played in the East—music that, at its best, had an essential translucency hitched to a swinging, occasionally outrightly forceful attack.

Rogers' arranging style, displayed on a record called *Modern Sounds* on Capitol, in performances at the Lighthouse and in subsequent recordings for both the Lighthouse and Contemporary labels, established the outlines of "West Coast Jazz."

In 1952, when Rogers and the Lighthouse group had become firmly established, another significant name entered the West Coast picture—Gerry Mulligan, the baritone saxophonist and arranger who had played a prominent role in Miles Davis' nonet and had written for and subsequently played with Claude Thornhill's orchestra. Mulligan had moved West from New York and had made the acquaintance of Richard Bock, a college student who had a part-time job doing publicity for a Los Angeles club, The Haig, and organizing Monday night jam sessions there. In June, 1952, Bock, who had been using Mulligan on his Monday night sessions, made arrangements for Mulligan to use a tape recorder at a friend's house so he could tape some performances with Jimmy Rowles, a pianist, Red Mitchell, a bassist, and Chico Hamilton, a drummer. Rowles, the pianist, did not arrive but Mulligan went ahead with the recordings with just the bassist and drummer. Subsequently Mulligan insisted on playing his Monday night sessions without a piano.

At these sessions, he usually played with Chet Baker, a

trumpeter, Bob Whitlock, a bassist, and Hamilton. After five Monday night sessions with his group, Mulligan decided it was ready to record and Bock once again borrowed his friend's tape machine and house. The two pieces recorded on this occasion, *Bernie's Tune* and *Lullaby of the Leaves,* were so successful that Bock decided to start a record company, Pacific Jazz, to release them. This release put Bock in the record business and established the Gerry Mulligan Quartet as a prime West Coast attraction.

The distinctive characteristic of this quartet was its long periods of simultaneous improvisation between Mulligan and Baker, whose playing on trumpet was based on the coolest, most withdrawn side of Miles Davis' work. Mulligan, similarly, was playing then in relatively low-keyed fashion, possibly because he was just emerging from a period in which his control of his horn had been somewhat uncertain. With both men playing duets and solos in this fashion, the effect seemed a perfect example of the cool sound.

"The feeling," said Bock, "was as if they were talking to each other on their horns, inter-weaving vocalized lines."

One aspect of the quartet that aroused great curiosity was the elimination of the piano. At first this caused consternation among many listeners. How could a jazz group play without a piano, they asked, until Mulligan pointed out that the earliest jazz bands, which were either marching or riding in a wagon, had not used a piano, either.

"The piano is an orchestra and, as such, naturally offers many wonderful possibilities, both as a solo instrument and also in conjunction with an ensemble," Mulligan also pointed out. "However, its use with the rhythm section, where its function is to 'feed' the chords of the progression to the soloist, has placed the piano in a rather uncreative and somewhat mechanical role. By eliminating this role from the piano in my group, I actually open whole new fields of exploration and possibilities when I do choose to use one. As for myself, I just don't consider the piano an indispensable part of the rhythm section. I think it is more habit than logic that it is accepted standard practice to use the piano thusly."

One of those who hailed Mulligan's position was Bill Russo who declared that "Mulligan has spared us the insufferable continuousness of the accompanying piano." This, Russo said, produced two equally important benefits.

"First is the less monotonous sound of a jazz group without a piano; second is the thinning out, the greater clarity so produced."

Although the Mulligan Quartet seemed to fit into the growing picture of an indigenously cool West Coast sound and despite Mulligan's earlier cool associations in the East, he has subsequently turned out to be almost the very opposite of the withdrawn, unemotional jazz musician identified with cool jazz. His playing frequently has much of the gutty, stomping fervor of prewar and pre-swing jazz which is combined with and conditioned by his awareness of many other facets of jazz. Dave Brubeck has said of Mulligan's playing that "you feel as if you were listening to the past, present and future of jazz all in one tune and yet it's done with such taste and respect that you're not even aware of a change in idiom."

Mulligan's catholic taste in jazz has been made evident not only by those whom he has listened to with interest and from whom he has learned—a list that includes Charlie Parker, Dizzy Gillespie and Lester Young along with Jack Teagarden, the Bob Crosby and Jimmie Lunceford bands, Duke Ellington and Ellington's baritone saxophonist,

Harry Carney, and onetime drummer Sonny Greer—but also by his propensity for sitting in with anyone, anywhere, any time, under almost any conditions. It was typical of Gerry Mulligan that he drove out on Long Island to the Great South Bay Jazz Festival in the summer of 1957, paid his way in as a spectator and, carrying his saxophone with him, wandered backstage where he nestled under the platform playing quietly along with every group on the program, from Dixieland to modern. He finally worked his way around to the front of the platform so he could sit in with the Fletcher Henderson Alumni Band which had been specially brought together for the festival.

Although Mulligan himself drew away from the cool confines, two members of his original group—Chet Baker and Chico Hamilton—continued to further the cool concept on the West Coast with groups of their own. But the original vitality with which this Coast cool school had been launched by the Rogers and Mulligan groups was soon vitiated—on one hand by Mulligan's personal development, on the other by a steady watering down of Rogers' writing and the writing of those who followed along the lines he had charted. By 1955 Mulligan noted that much of the West Coast jazz had acquired a sameness of sound, a neutral quality.

"It may be due to all the inter-recording of personnel being done here," he said, referring to the standard clique of musicians who made most of the records produced in the Los Angeles area. "I'd say a lot of the music from the Coast is lacking that stamp of spontaneity that is so important an element of jazz to me."

Miles Davis heard the same results but drew different conclusions.

"You know what's wrong with the music on the Coast?"

he asked one who sought his views. "Smog! I've heard a lot of bad music coming from the Coast. Some of the arrangements are good but they die because there are no soloists. You've got to have a good rhythm section and you have to have guys who fit together. Maybe the climate has something to do with the guys playing the way they do. I know it makes my eyes water."

The absence of viable soloists was a symptom not only of the diminishing value of West Coast jazz but of the general limitations of the cool school as a whole. Max Harrison, an English critic, in viewing the strengths and weaknesses of cool jazz, took cognizance of the fact that it was, to some extent, a reaction to the complexities of bop.

"Its exponents employed simpler melodic constructions, very relaxed rhythmic frameworks and a less dense harmonic structure," he asserted. "They played with less attack than their predecessors and used a paler, less emotional instrumental tone. Reactions are natural enough in some circumstances, but cool jazz failed to develop a group of soloists comparable to those of bop. As against this, the cool style did produce what were to remain for a number of years almost the only outstanding modern jazz arrangements."

FOUR

Re-evaluation

As a reaction, cool jazz soon showed signs of having swung too far away from the viable center of jazz. In its use of superficial effects simply for their own sake, the music was drained of its essential vitality and became increasingly effete. This direction was epitomized in the work of Chet Baker, the trumpeter in Gerry Mulligan's original quartet. Moving out of the quartet and on his own, the lackadaisical limpness in Baker's playing became more pronounced, although he was still capable of passages with some measure of intensity. But it was in the growing reputation that he acquired in the middle fifties as a vocalist that the complete dead end of coolness for the sake of coolness could be seen. Baker's singing was bloodless to the point of utter listlessness, his range was infinitesimal and the total effect was one of self-pitying moroseness.

In the face of this, a return toward—if not to—the lusty, outgoing essentials of jazz seemed inevitable. Jazz, throughout its relatively short history, had had a highly emotional core until the arrival of the cool school. The emotional basis for jazz had been implemented in the past by the fact that it was played as music for dancing. After World War

45

II, however, it became increasingly a music for listeners only. The excitement that was almost inevitable in a music that implied physical activity could now be drained from jazz without detracting from the interests of its audience. This the cool school proceeded to do. And then to overdo.

Two musicians played an essential, ground-breaking role in taking jazz back to its roots. One was Horace Silver, a pianist from Norwalk, Connecticut, who had the sort of grounding in jazz that was missing in most of the young musicians who grew up during the bop days of the forties. Silver was one of the few who knew that jazz had roots that went beyond Charlie Parker and Dizzy Gillespie.

"Perhaps some of the young musicians who put down the older men only started listening to jazz when Bird came," Silver once remarked. "But I was listening to jazz before I heard Bird and Diz. I've always been a record collector since I was about twelve and would always buy at least two or three records a week."

His interests were broad. He liked Basie's band and Ellington's but his favorite was Jimmie Lunceford's orchestra because of its superb section work. He bought records by Louis Jordan and Jay McShann, and by a variety of blues singers ranging from Joe Turner, Bea Booze, Lil Green and Memphis Minnie to Peetie Wheatstraw. Silver had loved the blues since his earliest memories of music and when he started to play the piano his early efforts were in boogiewoogie. Later he acquired some of Teddy Wilson's characteristics and tried—not too successfully, he says—to pick up some of Art Tatum's style. He added the tenor saxophone to his musical arsenal when he was in high school and was soon doing a respectable representation of Lester Young. Finally, when he was eighteen, he heard Bud Powell and he was still under the influence of

Powell when he first began to make his mark as a professional in jazz with Stan Getz's group in the early fifties.

As long as he remained at home listening to records,
Silver recalled several years later, all he did was copy whatever he heard on a record. Once he left Connecticut and
went on the road with Getz, he began to develop something
of his own. But then, after a year with Getz, he settled in
New York and went through a brief period of retrogres-
sion.

"There I was, suddenly thrown in among the guys who
had been my idols," he explained. "I found myself going
the way I had when I was just listening to records—I was
trying to play like whoever I heard. Until I made my first
records, I didn't know what I sounded like."

As he made more records, Silver became increasingly
aware of his own individuality as a pianist and, accordingly,
his personal approach became more apparent in his playing.

The source of jazz for Silver was the blues and, as his
attitude toward himself in relation to jazz took shape, his
playing clung closer and closer to his root source. His aim,
he has said, is to create "tunes with a blues feeling and a
hell of a beat and a melody that is meaningful." He first
began to attract wide attention with compositions that reflected these three points—*The Preacher, Doodlin', Señor
Blues.*

"I write the way I feel," Silver once said, "and I play the
same way."

Silver's way of playing is based on a punching, jabbing,
driving attack over a left hand that, as Shelly Manne has
said, is "sort of growling at you." Silver's performances are
as much physical as they are mental. A neatly dapper man
away from the piano, twinkling-eyed and gently spoken,

47

he attacks the keyboard with tremendous ferocity. Hunching over the keys, his arms splayed out akimbo, a long lock of black hair dancing in front of his face as perspiration trickles down his nose, chin and neck, he appears determined to beat the piano into submission as he builds his forcefully stated solos with directness and simplicity.

In New York, early in the fifties, Silver came together with another well-grounded musician who shared his views on the emotionally communicative nature of jazz. Art Blakey, a drummer, had managed to crowd an unusual range of jazz experience into the fifteen years that preceded his association with Silver. He made at least fleeting contact with the basic big band style as it was practiced in the twenties when he played with Fletcher Henderson's last big band in 1939. Later, in the forties, he was the drummer in the first big bop band, Billy Eckstine's, during the three years of its existence. He had also drummed in Lucky Millinder's band and for groups led by Mary Lou Williams and Buddy De Franco and, briefly in the late forties, had led a big band of his own which he called the Messengers.

Blakey provided whatever group he was in with a massive rhythmic foundation. His drumming has always had substance and body although he is capable of achieving subtle shadings within this context. One of his most notable devices is a press roll that develops such muscular, lifting strength that it seems to raise the entire band off the floor and launches any soloist who moves out from it with such velocity that he may have to scramble to maintain his musical footing.

Blakey and Silver got to know each other at the Monday night jam sessions held at Birdland in the early fifties and in 1952 they took part in some trio recordings released under Silver's name. Two years later, when Silver was

48

scheduled to record with a larger group, he chose Blakey as one of his sidemen along with Kenny Dorham, trumpet, Hank Mobley, tenor saxophone, and Doug Watkins, bass. They were all so pleased with the results of this session, released on Blue Note, that they decided to stay together as a co-operative group. They called themselves the Jazz Messengers, a name that went back to Blakey's abortive big band attempt in the forties. Blakey liked the name because of the parallel he saw between good jazz and the spirit of a church meeting.

"When I was a kid," Blakey explained to a *Down Beat* interviewer, "I went to church mainly to relieve myself of problems and hardships. We did it by singing and clapping our hands. We called this way of relieving trouble 'having the spirit hit you.' I get that same feeling, even more powerfully, when I'm playing jazz. You get the message when you hear the music. And when we're on the stand and we see that there are people in the audience who aren't patting their feet and who aren't nodding their heads to our music, we know we're doing something wrong. Because when we do get our message across, those heads and feet do move."

This was a form of direct communication that had been drained out of jazz by the cool musicians. Silver, like Blakey, was attracted to this basic, emotional approach and was pleased when their group was able to "reach way back and get that old-time gutbucket barroom feeling with just a taste of backbeat."

It is interesting to find that the writing of both Silver and of the contributors to the Miles Davis nonet was motivated to some extent by a desire to get away from the similarity of pattern which had proved a sufficient framework for the bop men.

"I started writing because I was sick and tired of the

49

same routine," Silver said. "Always some sort of a quick intro and then everybody would take one series of choruses after another and then maybe we'd all play one last fast chorus together. So I started making up little interludes to relieve the monotony. They'd be sort of little intros for each soloist. Then after that I'd write things for the horns and rhythm to play together in the background."

The raw emotionalism that appealed to both Blakey and Silver came out in ensemble and solo playing of tremendously driving force, often in hard, edgy playing by the saxophone and trumpet over a relentless rhythm foundation. In 1956 Silver left the Messengers to form his own group while the Messengers, with frequently changing personnel, have continued under Blakey's leadership. Both groups continued to play in much the same manner as the early Messengers—although with increasing polish and deftness as Silver's group grew older, and when Blakey, after a couple of years with a ragged, uncertain group, found sidemen such as Benny Golson and Lee Morgan who were capable of taking over the group's musical direction.

In the middle fifties the emotional zest of the church music that had so impressed Blakey was also making itself felt on jazz through other musicians who had lived in close proximity to it as children. Negro church music had been allied to jazz since its earliest days. It was shaped from the same sources that provided the basic ingredients for jazz. Jazz treatment of hymns was such a common part of New Orleans jazz sixty years ago that it remains to this day a basic part of the repertory of traditional jazz groups. The association between jazz and church music continued into the twenties, although in lesser degree. But the conjunction of the two still had much to offer as Bubber Miley, Duke Ellington's original growl trumpet star, showed in

1927 when he based *Black and Tan Fantasy* on the hymn, *Holy City*.

As jazz acquired more and more sophistication and lost contact with its sources, the association between church music and jazz all but disappeared during the thirties and forties. The two came together again only when the jazz musician found himself at a sterile dead end and consciously sought out the real core of his music. The prime association this time was with modern gospel song, a highly emotional style of singing that grew out of the work of the shouting preachers of the twenties and thirties. This was a more complex and highly developed form than the earlier jubilees and spirituals and it found its outlet mainly in the large cities of the North in Holiness and Pentecostal churches which had replaced tightly disciplined ritual with an emphasis on exuberance and freedom of expression.

A child growing up in the Negro section of a northern city did not need to be part of a churchgoing family to be familiar with this new gospel music. Walking along the streets, he could not avoid hearing it as it poured out of the neighborhood churches. He grew up absorbing by osmosis this compellingly rhythmic, often extravagantly flamboyant music.

"Where Bags really gets his rhythm," Dizzy Gillespie once said in explaining the essential origins of Milt Jackson, the vibraphonist, "is that his family's sanctified."

Gospel song itself had drawn on devices developed by some of the early jazz musicians and was, in fact, very closely associated with the blues. Thus when the gospel influence was joined to the conscious searching for the blues roots of jazz, the combination produced a music of highly volatile emotionality. Since the use of blue tonality is common to both gospel song and to the blues, the resultant blueness or, musically speaking, "dirtiness" became identified as "funk." Horace Silver has described funkiness as "a sort of lowdown blues feeling" and he cautioned against deliberately playing funky.

"You should play it how you feel," he said. "If it's in you to be funky, then it's in you. Some guys are real funky—take Milt Jackson, he's as funky as you can get."

But even for a basically funky musician, Silver warned, funk can only be part of the story.

"Even if you play a slow blues, you're not going to be funky all the time. You also have to play some hip lines, some snake changes. I mean crisscrossing, weaving your way through the chords with hip lines. It's all mixed in there together—funk and everything else."

One odd offshoot of the search for jazz roots that was leading most jazz musicians back to the blues and to the church was the effort of Jimmy Giuffre, who had been identified with the cool West Coast element, to make a similar exploration on his own terms. By the mid-fifties, Giuffre had come to the conclusion that "a lot of people are stuck with a modern feeling."

"If they're stuck with it," he said, "I think that's limiting. I feel we have to relax and come down to earth, lose this phony thing."

A phony thing that bothered Giuffre about his own work was an awareness that the musical ideas that were beginning to interest him "might be considered old-fashioned or blues."

"I used to wonder, 'What will the cats think? What will Miles think? What will Getz think?' But something strange happened. I began to hear it in the music of Horace Silver, in Gerry Mulligan, in . . . Bobby Brookmeyer. They were playing with this mood of the old-time blues. It has a

CHARLIE PARKER

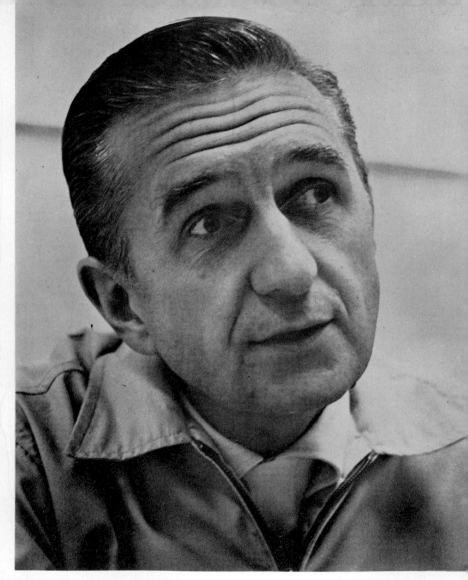

GIL EVANS

GERRY MULLIGAN *(left);* ZOOT SIMS *(right)*

fresh, new
ing with t

In his o
Giuffre sw
which had
which he
he felt te
as the whi
century w
the Negro
staccato,
music rat
emphasiz
were not

Blue Note Records

HORACE SILVER

cess and disappeared, apparently into the deeper recesses of Houston's Negro wards, until he was tracked down in 1957 by McCormick and Sam Charters, a jazz researcher and writer.

With Hopkins leading the way, some of the older blues men regained a measure of prominence—men such as Lonnie Johnson, Sunnyland Slim, Champion Jack Dupree, Memphis Slim, Roosevelt Sykes—while members of a younger generation also won a wider following—Muddy Waters, John Lee Hooker, Memphis Willie Borum among others.

The blues strain and the gospel strain came together in the singing and playing of Ray Charles, a blind pianist, saxophonist and vocalist who had moved, during the fifties, from the bouncing novelty manner of Louis Jordan to a pop style of performance in the manner of Nat "King" Cole, then to a rocking, blues-based rhythm and blues style and finally to a cross between blues and gospel.

Charles used the externals of gospel performance—the call-and-response pattern (with the assistance of four girls, The Raelettes) and the shouting, whooping, hollering, possessed fervor with which gospel singers are inclined to whip up the emotional climate as they develop their songs. But the internals, the lyrics, were in the worldly tradition of the blues. Charles has described his subject matter as "the things [that] concern the general Joe and his general problems."

"There are just four basic things," he said in outlining the topics of his songs. "Love, somebody running his mouth too much, having fun and jobs are hard to get."

Charles managed to project these traditional blues subjects with a heated intensity that was often electrifying in its impact by placing them in the framework commonly

55

associated with gospel song. There were those on both sides of this musical fence who disapproved of such cross-breeding. For one, Big Bill Broonzy, who, by the 1950's, had become an elder statesman among blues singers, declared that, although he sang church songs on occasion, he did not believe in mixing church music and the blues. Each in its own place, he said, and most church singers were inclined to agree. Mahalia Jackson, whose rich, vibrant voice had first made modern gospel song known to a wide audience, represented a relatively large number of her colleagues in refusing to sing the blues anywhere or to appear in clubs where the blues might normally be sung.

Most audiences were not inclined to be so finicky about these distinctions. They were swept up in Charles' dramatic presentation and were carried away more by the highly emotional nature of the music than by the meaning of the lyrics. Charles' appeal, critic Allan Morrison has pointed out, lay basically in his "funk," in the "mixture of raw emotional ingredients with which Charles can send the listener to the dizzy heights of joy or mire him in the pit of despair."

Charles himself had no gospel singing background but he admitted to being influenced by gospel material.

"I love a good gospel song if it's really soulful," he said. "And if you love something, then it's bound to rub off on you. . . . About the only records I buy myself are gospel records."

Through Charles, an emphasis on "soulfulness" or "soul" became a strong factor in the jazz of the late fifties. Essentially, this was a quality that had always played a notable role in jazz until the cool era—playing with meaningful conviction. But this projection of "soul," spurred by Charles' success, grew into a fad in the late fifties which, like most fads, retained only the most superficial aspects of the viable music on which it was based. The term "soul jazz" achieved wide currency and usually identified—on those occasions when there was any valid connection—minor-keyed, repetitious melodies played with a strong back beat.

A part of the flood of emotionalism that welled up in jazz following the re-examination of its blues roots was drained off by the exploitation of "soul jazz." But this scarcely touched the heart of the matter. At the same time that "soul jazz" was diluting the newly found emotionalism of jazz, this same emotionalism was providing a foundation for a group of musicians who were establishing one of the primary approaches to jazz as it was played during these years.

At the center of this approach were two tenor saxophonists, Sonny Rollins and John Coltrane. Both men brought back to this instrument a dark-toned warmth and richness that was characteristic of Coleman Hawkins but which had been shunted aside for many years by the dominance of Lester Young and Stan Getz and their followers. Rollins, in fact, began his career on tenor (he had first played alto) under the influence of both Hawkins and Young. In both cases, he was impressed by the bigness of the sound they produced even though the quality of their sounds was different. A later and more shaping influence was Charlie Parker.

Rollins was part of the so-called "hard bop" school that developed as the fifties rolled toward a midpoint, the school stemming from the driving intensity of men such as Horace Silver and Art Blakey. While Rollins' playing had a high emotional quotient, he was more directly concerned with shape and structure than were most of his hard bop colleagues. He is also one of the most self-critical musicians that jazz has seen. He has gone into retirement twice—once for a year, the second time for two years—in order to study his music and himself and to bring both into better alignment with his goals as a musician and as a man. His first retirement came at the end of 1954 after eight years of steady development as a tenor saxophonist. He had been making records off and on for six years (his first was with Babs Gonzales, a bop vocalist) but as he learned more and more through working with such men as Miles Davis, J. J. Johnson and Thelonious Monk, Rollins became increasingly dissatisfied with his recordings. He felt he had to get a better musical foundation before he could move on to the things he wanted to do, so he studied for a year with various teachers in Chicago, working as a day laborer to support himself.

He returned to an active career again in 1955 when he joined the Max Roach-Clifford Brown group. During the next three years Rollins rapidly developed into a saxophonist of commanding influence, playing in a clipped, curt, hard-driving style, using phrasing that in its harshness often edged over into satire. Despite his constantly growing stature, Rollins was again becoming dissatisfied with his playing and with the circumstances in which he found himself. To some degree, he felt, this stemmed from his joining the Roach-Brown group. He had only intended to fill in for a few weeks. But then he found himself staying and "I lost the thread of a lot of things I had planned to do."

When he became leader of his own group, he found that this was distracting him from his music.

"I never seem to have time to work, to practice and to write," he said in 1958. "Everything becomes secondary

HORACE SILVER

GERRY MULLIGAN *(left);* ZOOT SIMS *(right)*

to going to work every night and wondering how the band sounds and whether our appearances are okay."

At the same time he was having increasing difficulty in finding a group format in which he could play comfortably. His group at first was a quintet similar to the Brown-Roach setup (trumpet, tenor saxophone, piano, bass, drums). He soon dispensed with the trumpet because it distracted him. Next he dropped the piano.

"I was kind of disappointed with piano accompaniment," he admitted. "I was obliged to play *with* it. [Pianists] got in the way. They played too much. Their chords interrupted my train of thought. I ended up getting bugged at all piano players."

Ideally, said Rollins, he wanted to play unaccompanied tenor saxophone.

"I want to go on the concert stage and . . . be a soloist on the tenor, like Segovia does on the guitar," he said. "But it's very difficult because he has an instrument you can play chords on and I've got a wind instrument which is basically a single note instrument, although I can get two notes and approximate three."

Late in 1959, Rollins, riding the crest of his influence, again went into voluntary retirement. This time he remained out of sight for two years. Once more he was studying—classical piano, this time, and theory—and practicing his horn. He held his practice sessions on the footwalk of the Williamsburg Bridge over the East River, bordering Manhattan. It was an isolated spot—"you could see a person coming for five minutes before he got there," Rollins said —and he could play without the concern for other people that he felt when he practiced in his nearby apartment.

After two years of disciplining both his music and himself—as personal disciplines he gave up smoking and drinking and adopted a very simple manner of living—Rollins returned to public performance in the fall of 1961, not, he said, because he felt "really ready" to return but because "there is only a certain amount of work you can do by yourself—it doesn't mean anything until you do it on a stage for an audience."

Those who had expected a radical change in Rollins' style after two years found that, essentially, his playing was very much as it had been when he had retired, with one notable difference—much of the harshness had gone out of his tone.

"What had once sounded like music stemming from hate," wrote the New York *Herald Tribune*'s jazz critic, George Simon, "now seemed to come out of love."

Rollins agreed that his playing was warmer and more relaxed.

"You can't separate the two: living and playing," he said. "There'd been several things in my personal life I'd been unhappy about and they were affecting my music. So I took time out to get refreshed."

In this mood, Rollins continued his search for the means of achieving the greatest possible freedom within a disciplined and logical musical structure—in effect, trying to expand the free emotional values of jazz by maintaining a tight rein on the form within which they are expressed.

During the two years that Rollins took himself out of circulation, Coltrane's star was rising quickly. Coltrane had arrived among the hard-blowing saxophonists by a route very similar to Rollins'. Like Rollins, he had started on alto saxophone, later shifting to tenor. His early influences were Lester Young, Charlie Parker and Coleman Hawkins plus one that is not notably present in Rollins— Johnny Hodges. Coltrane's development was spurred by working with Monk and Davis and he has been as fascinated as Rollins by the potential of playing more than a single note at a time on a saxophone. Again, like Rollins, he had a period when he found that what he was playing clashed with the piano and, as a result, he frequently played with only bass and drum accompaniment.

But whereas Rollins' career followed a cumulatively developing line, Coltrane spent most of a decade in which he was known as a capable but in no way extraordinary saxophonist. During these years he worked in Dizzy Gillespie's big band, with Earl Bostic's rhythm and blues group and with the band led by Johnny Hodges during his brief withdrawal from Duke Ellington's band in the fifties.

When Coltrane joined Miles Davis' Quintet in 1955, he began to move out of the relative rut that he had followed during his early years. His musical curiosity appears to have been primed by his contact with Davis and later by a brief stretch with Thelonious Monk. It was Monk, among others, who interested Coltrane in attempting to play chords on his saxophone. He returned to Davis in 1958, a period when his playing was marked by very long phrases played at extremely rapid tempos, an effect characterized by the leading authority on modern saxophonists, Ira Gitler, as "sheets of sound." In actuality, according to Coltrane, this was the result of his attempts to play three chords on one and, since he tended to play the entire scale of each chord, they were usually played very fast and gave the glimmering effect of a wavering sheet of sound. During the early stages of this period, Coltrane played with what the English jazz observer, Michael Gibson, has described as "a surfeit of passion at the expense of subtlety."

It was in 1960, with Rollins out of the spotlight, that Coltrane came into his own. He had his own group by then and was moving completely in his own direction instead of being conditioned by another dominant personality such as Davis or Monk. He had refined his "sheets of sound" technique to such a point that he could be more selective in building his solos. And he had found in the soprano saxophone a second instrument on which he could play with all the power and searing emotionalism that he exhibited on tenor saxophone. There were harsh and biting overtones in much of what he played and, particularly on the soprano saxophone, he was fond of a repetitiously wailing, keening effect. To some listeners this made his music sound "angry" or "tortured." To others it was "spiritual," "overpowering."

"All a musician can do," said Coltrane in considering these diverse reactions, "is to get closer to the sources of nature and so feel that he is in communion with the natural laws. Then he can feel that he is interpreting them to the best of his ability and can try to convey that to others."

The need to get close to the source was a dominant theme among the jazzmen of the late fifties who were emerging from the hard bop line ("I've found that you've got to look back at the old things and see them in a new light," said Coltrane). This, and a search for freedom of musical expression, appear as a tandem in their motivations time and time again.

But while Rollins and Coltrane sought freedom within a formalized structure, a less confining form of freedom seemed to be the goal of the most thoroughgoing individualist that jazz produced in the late fifties. Ornette Coleman, a mild-mannered, somewhat saintly looking man, exploded suddenly on the New York jazz scene late in the fall of 1959 just as Sonny Rollins was removing himself to the sidelines. Coleman had been preceded to New York by a single LP made in California and high words of praise by musicians who had heard him. He played a white plastic saxophone and when he blew into it a listener might hear anything from the most essential root blues to the most discordantly far-out expression with all degrees of shrieks, wails and squawks in between. Pianist John Lewis of the Modern Jazz Quartet hailed him as "the only really new thing in jazz since the mid-forties." Classical composer and critic Virgil Thomson, going back even farther, said Coleman was the first new thing he had heard in jazz since Louis Armstrong.

Pianist André Previn called him "an unmitigated bore." Leonard Bernstein called him a genius. Dizzy Gillespie listened to Coleman's group and asked, "Are you cats serious?" Trumpeter Maynard Ferguson accused him of having bad intonation and bad technique.

Whitney Balliett of *The New Yorker* described a Coleman solo that "began with a fusillade of shrieks, blats and groans, abruptly fell into quick, graceful sotto voce passages—passages that gave the effect of test runs not yet ready for public use—broken by outcroppings of human-voice sounds, then gave way to a long series of figures delivered in a straight, thick-textured melodic manner that disconcertingly recalled the Stone Age saxophones of Guy Lombardo."

During another Coleman solo, Balliett heard "a concatenation of moans, yelps, frenzied twitterings (birds fleeing a great storm), bathtub arias, Oriental singsong effects, sudden soft plaintive lyrical passages that take the emotions by surprise, scurrying sounds and shrieks."

George Crater, a columnist in *Down Beat* magazine,

wondered if an evening of listening to Ornette Coleman was covered by Blue Cross.

Coleman himself remained calm in the face of all this hullabaloo.

"I haven't heard one person yet who can explain what I'm doing," he said. "People laugh at me, shake their heads. But I won't let any of that affect me. . . . Most people fail to hear what is being played at the *moment* it is being played. They pay more attention to behavior and what they see than to what is happening musically. I'm beginning where Charlie Parker stopped. Parker's melodic lines were placed across ordinary chord progressions. My melodic approach is based on phrasing and my phrasing is an extension of how I hear the intervals and pitch of the tunes I play."

Coleman is a self-taught saxophonist who launched his musical career by misunderstanding an instruction book and, as a consequence, taught himself wrong. It was two years before he discovered his mistake. He left his native Fort Worth with Pee Wee Crayton's rhythm and blues band but Crayton dropped him off in Los Angeles in 1950 because, as Coleman explained, "It got so he was paying me not to play." For the next eight years Coleman shuttled back and forth between Los Angeles and Fort Worth, arousing nothing but antagonism whenever he attempted to play, so he did most of his playing alone wherever he happened to be living. Howard Rumsey, who led the group at the Lighthouse at Hermosa Beach in those years, remembers Coleman then.

"Everybody—the musicians, I mean—would panic when you'd mention Ornette," he recalled. "People would laugh when his name was brought up."

By 1957 Coleman was beginning to attract a few adherents, youngsters who were as unknown as he was. They included Don Cherry, a trumpet player, Don Payne, a bassist, and Billy Higgins, a drummer. (Cherry and Higgins were members of Coleman's quartet when he came East in 1959.) The next year Coleman gained another adherent in Red Mitchell, the bassist, and through Mitchell got his first recording opportunity. Mitchell had been impressed by some of Coleman's original tunes and suggested he take them to Lester Koenig, head of Contemporary Records. When Coleman arrived with his tunes, Koenig took him to a piano and asked him to play them.

"Ornette then said he couldn't *play* the piano," Koenig later told John Tynan of *Down Beat*. "I asked him, 'How did you hope to play your tunes for me if you can't play piano?' So he took out his plastic alto and began to play."

Koenig liked both the tunes and the way Coleman played them and offered him a chance to record. A short time later John Lewis of the Modern Jazz Quartet heard him at an after-hours jam session in Terry Lester's Jazz Cellar in Los Angeles and was so impressed ("He's an extension of Bird") that he arranged for both Coleman and Cherry to attend the School of Jazz at Lenox, Massachusetts, in the summer of 1959. At the school Coleman and Cherry became the focus of special interest to such an extent that Bob Brookmeyer, the valve trombonist, who was teaching at the school that summer, became incensed at the attention they were getting. This, coupled with the fact that he had to listen to their music day and night, drove him to quit the faculty.

"I used to scream out of my window, 'Damn it, tune up!' as these cats would play evenings downstairs," he said. However, when Coleman's Quartet began playing regularly at the Five Spot in New York a few months later, Brookmeyer revised his opinion.

"I've learned a lesson in tolerance," he admitted. "I'm

sure that my rejection of this music was based simply on intolerance of something I was not familiar with."

The basis of Ornette Coleman's approach to jazz is freedom—freedom from the limitations imposed by adhering to a given key, given harmonic changes or a given rhythm. Yet within this freedom as analytical a listener as Gunther Schuller has found "a deep inner logic, based on subtleties of reaction, subtleties of timing and color that are . . . quite new to jazz."

Music, Coleman has said, is for our feelings.

"The most beautiful feeling I get out of listening to jazz is to have my feelings take the shape of the notes," he has declared. "When this happens, it will always have a beautiful and clear meaning to me. But if you have to sit down and figure out every note resolving to its right place, then the natural feeling you have for the music will be left unexploited."

Coleman's attempt to exploit his "natural" feeling for music broke with tradition to such an extent that his music struck many listeners as outlandish, a reaction that had also been produced by two earlier individualists of the fifties whose music was strongly marked by their uniquely expressive personalities.

Thelonious Monk was not, properly speaking, a musical product of the fifties. He had been the pianist in Kenny Clarke's house band at Minton's in 1941 when bop was being brewed. It was Monk who joined with Dizzy Gillespie then in dreaming up complex variations on chords to scare away the "no-talent" guys who insisted on sitting in.

But Monk was not part of the bop movement. He was his own man right from the start and as bop formulated around Parker and Gillespie, Monk moved along in an orbit of his own.

"They think different, harmonically," he once said in explaining the difference between himself and the bop musicians he had worked with at Minton's. "They play mostly stuff that's based on the chords of other things, like the blues and *I Got Rhythm*. I like the whole song, melody and chord structure, to be different. I make up my own chords and melodies."

Monk's insistence on making up his own chords and melodies helped to make him seem particularly weird in a jazz world that, to some listeners, already appeared weird enough without going as far afield as Monk did. Monk, however, views his work and all the other aspects of his existence as completely rational. When he appeared as a guest with a lecturer on jazz at Columbia University, he was asked to demonstrate "some of your weird chords."

Monk bridled.

"What do you mean, weird?" he complained. "They're perfectly logical."

Monk has been able to remain relatively unaffected by the world around him—by acceptance or nonacceptance, by the vagaries of employment—because he lived at home with his parents for many years and consequently always had food and shelter. Later, after his marriage, he found in his wife, Nellie, a devoted shield against worldly intrusions. Through the forties and into the early fifties, Monk worked only sporadically and was known primarily through his recordings. Not before the mid-fifties, roughly fifteen years after he began to be known in jazz circles through his work at Minton's, was he heard regularly enough, both in person and on records, to break through the aura of mystery that had hidden him from a wider audience. Finally, his angular, hauntingly off-center melodies began to find a growing body of appreciative listeners.

Monk is a stocky, bearlike man who hunches his huge shoulders over the keyboard, his fingers spread out flat as he plays. Sometimes he uses his entire forearm or elbow to play a cluster of notes. Sometimes he stops playing entirely and just sits at the piano while someone else solos. Sometimes he gets up and goes into a shuffling, ecstatic dance which may be either a sign of pleasure or an effort to get the group into the proper tempo.

To Monk, jazz is a perpetual adventure.

"I'm after new chords, new ways of syncopating, new figurations, new runs," he has said. "How to use notes differently. That's it. Just using notes differently."

By this Monk does not mean placing notes in different combinations or contexts but actually *using* them in a different fashion—that is, getting a different sound with them. Dick Katz, another pianist, has noted that the special tone qualities that Monk gets out of a piano are an important part of the success of what he does.

"He taught me one of his compositions note for note," Katz said in explaining the effect that Monk's personal sound has, "but I couldn't make it *sound* the way it was supposed to."

Wry wit colors almost everything Monk plays.

"There is something almost surgical about the manner in which he will take a standard tune, examine it, and strip it of its conventional trappings and associations, investing it with a new power that is all his own," Michael James, a critic, has observed. "Beneath his fingers *Sweet and Lovely* is shorn of all cloying sentiment; one might say with some degree of justification that it becomes a satire of itself."

A strong feeling for rhythm is also present in Monk's work. Everything about it, in fact, is strong. Charlie Rouse, the tenor saxophonist who has worked with Monk since 1959, discovered the definitely masculine character of

Monk's music when he joined Monk's group after being co-leader with Julius Watkins, a French hornist, of the Jazz Modes.

"You can't play soft with Monk," Rouse declared. "You have to be as strong and dynamic as he is. When I first came with the band he said, 'Rouse, you're not playing with a French horn now. You're out there alone.' He'd swallow me up if I didn't play strong."

The other great jazz individualist of the fifties, bassist Charlie Mingus, has a musical personality that is at least as strong as Monk's but he projects it with a great deal more ferocity. Where Monk is inclined to shut out anything that bothers him, Mingus is more apt to swing out wildly and vigorously. He is a highly volatile man, and his music is an expression of this volatility.

"Music is his primary, essential means of communication with others," Nat Hentoff has observed. "He tells in his work of his fears, his loves, his inflammable conflicts, his night-to-night battles to find and be himself. Since his music emerges from specific emotional needs, form in his work always follows function. His first concern is with what he wants to say, and the subject matter determines the way the piece is then structured."

Mingus has been engaged in an effort to communicate himself through music since the end of his high school career just before World War II when he was composing pieces that gained him a reputation as an *avant-garde* jazz musician when they were finally heard more than ten years later. "I'm not an experimenter," Mingus said then, in answering charges of *avant gardism*. "I wrote these things ten years ago."

His earliest influences were church music and Duke Ellington. Then, he said, "writing came natural."

"I heard things in my head—then I'd find it on the

69

piano. Jazz to me was Duke and the church but I thought all music was one—jazz, symphony. That's the bag I was working out of then."

Subsequently, his experiences as a sideman brought him in contact with an amazingly wide range of jazz styles and outlooks. He has worked with Kid Ory and Louis Armstrong, with Lionel Hampton and Duke Ellington, with Red Norvo and Charlie Parker and Art Tatum. In the fifties he organized a Jazz Workshop through which passed an astonishing number of bright—often brilliant—new, young jazz musicians from whom Mingus was able to draw a personal interpretation of his own openly emotional style of playing. At the same time, Mingus' means of expression turned away from his early dalliance with arranged music to freely organized pieces drenched in church feeling and the blues.

"I 'write' compositions on mental score paper," he once explained. "Then I lay out the composition part by part to the musicians. I play them the 'framework' on piano so that they are all familiar with my interpretation and feeling and with the scale and chord progressions to be used. Each man's particular style is taken into consideration. They are given different rows of notes to use against each chord but they choose their own notes and play them in their own style, from scales as well as chords, except where a particular mood is indicated. In this way I can keep my own compositional flavor in the pieces and yet allow the musicians more individual freedom in the creation of their own group lines and solos."

Jimmy Knepper, a trombonist who has been through the Mingus workshop, found Mingus' compositional approach challenging and stimulating.

"It takes a little while to get in the spirit of some of his tunes," Knepper reported. "They're kind of strange at first. He's written tunes—he says he hears them like this—where all of a sudden there's a two-beat insert. So the soloist has to sort of hang on. The drummer plays it—he's straight—but the horns have to stand around and mark time waiting for the bridge. But once you learn his tunes, once you *feel* how they should be played, they come easily. He expects quick results but understands the musician's problems. And he doesn't impose his own ideas on you but wants individual interpretations."

Despite his extremely personal approach to music, Mingus has served as a somewhat unexpected synthesizer of the elements that made up one of the two major jazz streams of the fifties. In his fervent music one finds the renewed interest in the basic roots of jazz represented in the blues and in gospel music, one hears the driving explosiveness of the hard bop men and there is also the search for freedom—both in individual and group expression—that lies at the heart of Ornette Coleman's efforts. And yet with it all, a mercurial curiosity and adventurousness remains that is peculiarly Mingusian. One of his efforts to break through formalized limitations was something he called "rotary perception" in which, he said, the musician, thinking of the beat as circular, could come in anywhere within the four beats of a measure and still be in the right place.

"It isn't easy," Mingus admitted. "But then I always wanted to walk on water."

FIVE

Intellectualization

Early jazz, which was primarily an expression of emotions, inevitably drew the attention of those who, seeing in it only disorder—albeit, well-meaning disorder—instinctively sought to give it some sort of order. "Order," in these circumstances, normally meant the application of the rules and regulations of Western European music.

In some cases, this took the form of absorption or borrowing, as when such composers as Igor Stravinsky, Eric Satie, George Auric, Paul Hindemith, John Alden Carpenter, Aaron Copland and Darius Milhaud used elements drawn from jazz in typically Western European compositions. Aside from Milhaud's *Creation du Monde,* none of this borrowing produced particularly noteworthy results.

The more normal procedure was the attempt to clothe jazz—or what purported to be jazz—in the trappings of European music. In the twenties, when a wide audience was first becoming aware of jazz, this was the approach of Paul Whiteman who was going to "make a lady out of jazz." Whiteman's Aeolian Hall concert in 1924, which was climaxed by the première of Gershwin's *Rhapsody in Blue,* began with a group of short selections in which it was

Whiteman's intent to show "the tremendous strides which have been made in popular music from the day of discordant jazz, which sprang into existence about ten years ago from nowhere in particular, to the really melodious music of today." He demonstrated these "tremendous strides" by playing pseudo-symphonic arrangements of *A Pretty Girl Is Like a Melody, Limehouse Blues,* and *To a Wild Rose.*

Whiteman's swollen orchestra continued to play similarly flowery pastiches through the twenties but they were swept from the music scene in the thirties by the direct, unfussy attack of the swing bands which had no patience with extraneous filigree. Through the thirties and early forties jazz was spared further "improvements" of this sort although there were classical reflections in the chamber jazz efforts of a group called the New Friends of Rhythm.

After the war, a new type of personality came into jazz —the conservatory-trained musician whose primary interest lay in jazz although he had been trained in European music. These young musicians differed from the Whiteman school of symphonicizers in that, instead of hiding jazz under a "respectable" coating, their interest usually lay in expanding the scope of jazz by means of the forms and techniques developed by European music. At the same time the gap between the jazz musician and the non-jazz musician that had existed in Whiteman's day narrowed considerably because postwar jazz musicians, unlike their predecessors who often had little facility at reading, were increasingly well schooled (particularly as the result of the educational opportunities offered to war veterans by the GI Bill of Rights) while symphony musicians had had some unavoidable contacts with jazz while they were growing up. Thus, it was becoming possible for a composer with jazz

73

intentions to write something with the reasonable expectation that it would both be read properly and played with jazz expression.

In the immediate postwar years the outstanding example of a conservatory-trained musician who worked in the jazz milieu was Ralph Burns, a pianist and arranger in Woody Herman's band, who wrote *Summer Sequence* for the Herman band. From the other side of the fence, Igor Stravinsky also wrote a work for the Herman band, *Ebony Rhapsody*, which was neither notable Stravinsky nor notable jazz. But most of the effort to add intellectual qualities to the basic good-time nature of jazz during these years centered on Stan Kenton's orchestra.

Kenton, a pianist and arranger, had come to attention in the fading days of the swing era with what was, essentially, a big swing band. He had worked as a pianist on the West Coast for six years before he made his debut as a bandleader in Balboa Beach, California, in May, 1941. Kenton's arranging style stemmed to a great extent from that used by Jimmy Lunceford's band. He got a big, fat sound from his reeds, capped his climaxes with screaming trumpets and spread his ensemble sounds over a wide expanse. Through the war years, the band's popularity spread, helped by the work of two singers, Anita O'Day and June Christy, and by the distinctively full sound that Kenton got from all his sections.

In 1947 he undertook a concert tour, offering what he called "A Concert in Progressive Jazz." This leaned heavily on arrangements following the general pattern established by Kenton, but written by Pete Rugolo, whose relationship to Kenton at that time was much like that of Billy Strayhorn to Duke Ellington. (The term "progressive jazz" has since been used broadly and loosely by some people to identify almost any form of postwar jazz. However, the

only time it has had a specific meaning was as an identi-
fication of the music that Kenton played on this particular
tour.)

After resting up during the winter of 1948–1949, Kenton
began laying his plans for another tour to start in the fall
of 1949. The first tour had whetted his concert appetite
and he launched into what he has called "a highly experi-
mental" period. The band he assembled for this second
tour consisted of forty pieces including a sixteen-piece
string section, two French horns and a tuba. He discarded
the "Progressive Jazz" label in favor of a new one—"Innovations in Modern Music." And he loaded his program
with compositions that often had scarcely any discernible
relation to jazz.

"For me," jazz writer Bill Coss reported after hearing
Kenton's "Innovations" concert at Carnegie Hall, "Stan
was way out, not in jazz but in some conglomeration of
early twentieth century 'classical' music superimposed on
a heavy beat."

Kenton, however, saw his music as a reflection of the
times.

"People hear music," he declared, "and they don't know
what the hell they like about it but it creates a certain
turmoil, a certain insecurity, certain things that are with
us today."

For the next few years Kenton persisted in his "experi-
mental" works, reaching an extreme in a piece by Robert
Graettinger, a young composer who wrote almost exclusively for the Kenton band. Graettinger's *City of Glass*
contains, as Gunther Schuller has pointed out, "almost no
jazz material, certainly not from any conventional point of
view, but it came to be confused with jazz by many people
because it was performed and recorded by Stan Kenton
and his orchestra."

While he was fomenting this confusion, Kenton became a highly controversial figure. Arthur Fiedler, conductor of the Boston Pops Orchestra, called him the most important link between jazz and the classics. Nesuhi Ertegun, a jazz enthusiast of long standing who then owned a record shop in Los Angeles, Kenton's home territory, called him "the loudest, emptiest sound in American music."

"Stan is supposed to be a very sincere person," mused Lennie Tristano, who was a fairly controversial musician himself, "but I wonder if he's really with the music, enjoys it himself. Personally, even when I enjoy his things I still don't think they're jazz."

Albert J. McCarthy, an English critic, declared that Kenton's music screams "because it can make its point no other way."

"Some of the wise boys who say my music is loud, blatant and that's all," Kenton has pointed out, "should see the faces of the kids who have driven a hundred miles through the snow to see the band . . . to stand in front of the stand in an ecstasy all their own."

By the mid-fifties, and particularly after Graettinger's death in 1957, Kenton had moved away from the classical derivatives and settled into the main current of jazz although his bands continued to play with typical Kentonian fustian. Long before then, however, the classical influences on jazz had changed from Kenton's emphasis on twentieth century European mannerisms to the devices of an earlier day—to the rondo, the fugue and to counterpoint which had all but been eliminated from jazz by the unison ensembles of the bop musicians. Nor were the European influences displayed so blatantly as they had been in previous efforts.

The door to this intellectual approach to jazz was opened

by Dave Brubeck, a pianist whose intentions were not primarily intellectual but whose background and musical habits lent a suggestion of culture to his performances. Brubeck had enrolled in college with the intention of becoming a veterinarian but he soon switched to music and studied with Darius Milhaud at Mills College in California. In 1946 he was one of the founders of a co-operative octet formed to play jazz compositions written by its members. Five members of the octet had studied counterpoint, fugue and composition with Milhaud. It was an exploratory group that played only on the Mills campus until 1949 when it was presented to the general public for the first time. In 1950, when the octet was recorded, Paul Desmond, an alto saxophonist who was a member of the group, pointed out in the notes accompanying the disc that the music contained "the vigor and force of simple jazz, the harmonic complexities of Bartok and Milhaud, the form (and much of the dignity) of Bach, and at times the lyrical romanticism of Rachmaninoff."

This giddy stew was too rich for the 1950 record buyer and the octet disintegrated. Meanwhile, Brubeck had been leading a trio that worked occasionally—so occasionally that Brubeck supported himself for a while by selling sandwiches in office buildings in San Francisco. In 1951 he formed his quartet and, with the help of his wife, booked the group in an area that was relatively untouched by regular booking agencies—college campuses. By persistent effort, Brubeck built up a college following for his quartet which proved to be the foundation for his success.

Why did Brubeck appeal so strongly to this audience? In general, the collegiate knowledge of jazz at that time was limited to Dixieland played by tired and rather sloppy groups. In contrast to the noisy clichés of these groups,

Brubeck offered a mixture of excitement, deft individual interplay and an aura of culture. This was respectable jazz with roots in Milhaud rather than New Orleans bordellos. Brubeck has made a point of the pioneering value of his invasion of colleges.

"I know that at colleges where we've played, they've hired other [jazz] groups because they liked us," he told the jazz writer, Ralph J. Gleason. "The fan mail frequently mentions how they have become interested in jazz through us, even though they never liked it before."

The fact that Brubeck appealed to an audience that had never liked jazz before has its significance, for Brubeck was unlike anything that had turned up in jazz before. Nat Hentoff has spoken of Brubeck's "fierce aloneness in jazz" and has described his style as a "uniquely personal combination of Milhaud-like classical influences and unparalleled selected influences from one part of the jazz tradition."

By 1952 Brubeck's quartet had become sufficiently successful to come to the attention of *Time* magazine. A *Time* reporter raised the question of Brubeck's influences—were they really classical or jazz?

"When I play jazz I am influenced by classical music," Brubeck declared. "And when I compose I am influenced by jazz."

Two years later Brubeck received the ultimate *Time* accolade—his picture on the cover. His records were selling like pop hits and jazz critics were taking an increasingly dim view of his piano style. He was accused of "pounding interminably like a man breaking rocks with a sledge." His playing was "pretentious and non-swinging, a heavy-handed unrelenting succession of block chords."

In an analysis in *Metronome* magazine of the playing of the Brubeck quartet, Al Zeiger pointed out that "Brubeck's use of high-powered, dissonant chords is taken from the harmonic language of the modern contemporary composers. The melody is outlined in a continuous block of sound rather than in a single note line. . . . The quartet's use of the contrapuntal idea is far from modern. . . . The lines are diatonic rather than chromatic and there is a close adherence to eighteenth century contrapuntal principles."

"If one is unaware of form, inversions, dissonance, chord changes, rhythmic subtlety and thematic development," Zeiger concluded, "he is missing the crux of what Dave Brubeck and his group have to offer."

Since Brubeck's appeal has been primarily to a mass audience rather than to the specialized audience that might appreciate these technical points, it must be assumed that Brubeck has been able to gain and retain his vast following despite the fact that they are missing the crux of what he has to offer.

Although the Brubeck quartet developed largely outside the familiar jazz patterns, the Modern Jazz Quartet, which also made extensive use of classical devices, was a product of the mainstream of jazz in the late forties. The quartet, made up of John Lewis, pianist and musical director, Milt Jackson, vibes, Percy Heath, bass, and Kenny Clarke, drums (replaced in 1955 by Connie Kay), had its roots in Dizzy Gillespie's second big band, the one that he led from 1946 to 1950. Lewis, Jackson and Clarke were members of this band off and on from 1946 to 1948. Later, they frequently worked together, with Percy Heath on bass, as the Milt Jackson Quartet. The group began recording as the Modern Jazz Quartet in 1952 but it was two years before it was able to work regularly under this title.

As musical director, Lewis brought to the group's repertory an interest in the use of seventeenth and eighteenth century classical baroque forms. He was particularly interested in the fugue and in the quartet's early years much of the original material that Lewis wrote for the group had some fugal element. There were some objections from jazz followers to the formality in which Lewis cloaked the group's performances. It was often said that, of the two soloists in the group—Lewis and Jackson—Jackson was the more vitally swinging jazz musician and that he was being stifled in the contexts that Lewis established for the quartet.

Superficially, this may have been true at the time, for Lewis was then going through the process of learning how to use such devices as the fugue in terms that were more jazz-oriented than classical, and his personal style as a pianist was still evolving, whereas Jackson was already established as a strongly individual and capable jazz performer. There was disagreement, too, within the group regarding general policy. Clarke favored the generally accepted jazz approach—loosely organized, individualistic—as opposed to the formality that interested Lewis. It was as a result of this difference of opinion that Clarke left in 1955 and was replaced by Kay. In the next few years the quartet became one of the most smoothly functioning groups that had ever appeared in jazz as Lewis developed into a more positively swinging pianist (in a way that was uniquely his own) and the group as a whole mastered the technique of translating forms of all sorts into viable jazz terms.

Although there continued to be some critical resistance to Lewis' musical policies (in 1960 Whitney Balliett, writing in *The New Yorker,* referred to "the soft, powdered salon numbers composed by Lewis, which are all rustle and no muscle"), yet the development of both Lewis and the group was generally acknowledged (and remarks about the stifling of Jackson were heard less frequently possibly because, in the course of ten years, Jackson had given no indication of feeling stifled and seemed, if anything, to be a more buoyantly swinging musician than he had been before). The advancement was apparent both in the quartet's performances and in Lewis' handling of his material.

Noting that the quartet's first fugue, *Vendome,* sounds "like an 'exercise' as first recorded" and that although a later re-recording is "pretty jazzy but no more successful," the American critic Martin Williams has pointed to their second fugue, *Concorde,* as a turning point, for it was followed by "specifically jazz fugues"—*Versailles* and *Three Windows*—which "no longer remind us of Bach or the practice room but are vehicles for creative collective jazz improvisation."

The element of collective improvisation was one of the most important jazz aspects of the quartet's work. Once a mainstay of any jazz performance, collective improvisation had been thrust farther and farther into the jazz background by the increasing attention given to the soloist until, with the use of unison ensembles by bop musicians, it disappeared entirely. Max Harrison notes that while the quartet's jazz is "at times the most complex on the contemporary scene, it is also among the most spontaneous." He has further remarked on the fact that the episodes in their fugues are improvised and are based on predetermined harmonic sequences, and that a considerable part of the counterpoint in their other pieces is also improvised.

"Thus," he asserted, "the quartet has brought about a rebirth of the collective improvisation that . . . has been conspicuously absent from later phases [of jazz]."

The accumulation of various ways of making use of aspects of both the classical tradition of European music

81

and of jazz within a single context began to have a mush-
rooming effect in the mid-fifties as an increasing number
of composers and musicians were attracted to it. The interest came from both sides of the musical street. While
the Modern Jazz Quartet was grappling with its fugues,
Rolf Liebermann attempted to join his contemporary
European background with jazz in his *Concerto for Jazz
Band and Symphony Orchestra,* and Leonard Bernstein
and the New York Philharmonic commissioned works
by Teo Macero and William Russo, both of whom had
jazz backgrounds. One of the most significant steps in
advancing this fusion was the commissioning of several
works in this developing métier by the 1957 Brandeis
University Festival of Arts. The composers commissioned
were three from the jazz world—George Russell, Charlie
Mingus and Jimmy Giuffre—two from the world of contemporary European music—Harold Shapero and Milton
Babbitt—and one, Gunther Schuller, who was at home in
both worlds.

Largely because of this ambivalence, Schuller soon became a leading force in the development of a new musical
genre which, as he described it, attempted to fuse "the
improvisational spontaneity and rhythmic vitality of jazz
with the compositional procedures and techniques acquired in Western music during seven hundred years of
musical development." During a lecture shortly after the
Brandeis Festival he coined the term "third stream music"
to identify this genre—a music that was neither jazz nor
"classical" but which drew on elements of both.

This was a musical development that Dave Brubeck had
seen coming several years earlier, at a time when he himself
had not yet had any notable success.

"The future American composer," Brubeck wrote in

an article in *Down Beat* in 1950, "will write music which must be interpreted with an understanding of jazz—its particular spirit as well as its peculiar techniques of phrasing, tonal color and instrumental range. The jazz musician is not in the position to interpret this music, even though he may be more akin to it in spirit, because he has not yet gained the necessary familiarity with musical notation and other intellectual factors in musicianship. The symphony musician is handicapped by his inability to feel the complex rhythmic changes, unique phrasing, and the peculiar timbres of jazz. If the American composer is going to reflect successfully his background in his music, the instrumentalist of the future must have gained knowledge of both techniques."

Schuller was a veritable prototype of the new musician envisioned by Brubeck. He grew up with a classical training and a close interest in jazz. For two years he played French horn in the Cincinnati Symphony Orchestra and for ten years was first French horn in the Metropolitan Opera Orchestra. At the same time he played on some of the recordings by the Miles Davis nonet that marked the so-called birth of cool jazz. As a composer he also worked in both fields although his jazz compositions rarely plunged completely into jazz. They were more inclined to hug the fringes of the new third stream of music.

Of the pieces commissioned by the Brandeis Festival, the one generally considered most successful was George Russell's *All About Rosie*. Russell was something of an oddity in the third stream area for, unlike most of the third streamers, who had had considerable musical education, Russell was largely a self-taught musician. As a child in Ohio he was interested in jazz and learned to play drums. His first real musical training came when, at nineteen, he contracted tuberculosis and was sent to a sanitarium. There, another patient taught him how to write arrangements. After his release from the sanitarium, Russell wrote for Benny Carter and Earl Hines and became interested in the bop activities in New York in the mid-forties. When he suffered a relapse and spent another sixteen months in the hospital, he spent the time developing a new approach to tonality. For the first five months of this hospital stay, he was limited to strict bed rest and he could only think about music. During the remaining eleven months he was able to use the piano in the hospital library and he devoted himself to intensive research into tonality; research which led him to be highly impressed by the logic of the Lydian scale.

In 1950 Russell began a period of three years devoted to the development of a thesis on "The Lydian Concept of Tonal Organization." And for two years after that he composed in terms of the Lydian Concept to illustrate his theory. This concept was later developed into the Lydian Chromatic Concept of Tonal Organization, a twelve-tone concept based on the grading of the intervals on the basis of their close-to-distant relationship to a central tone.

"It isn't a *system*," Russell has declared, "but a way to think about music which, when fully understood, lends a disciplined freedom to the composer and/or the improvisor. It can't provide the intangibles—the up-from-the-inside cry of Billie Holiday or the emotional charge of Bird; it is only a tool with which to work. The final component—involvement of the human being on an emotional level—can make it complete."

In developing this theory and composing for it, Russell has admitted to a *mélange* of influences including Alban Berg, Gerry Mulligan, Igor Stravinsky, Gil Evans, Stefan Wolpe and George Handy. Pan-tonal and pan-rhythmic structures for improvisation have increasingly attracted his interest, for he believes that "jazz will by-pass atonality because jazz actually has roots in folk music, and folk music is scale-based music; and atonality negates the scale." The answer, he believes, lies in pan-tonality.

"The basic folk nature of the scales is preserved," he has explained, "and yet because you can be in any number of tonalities at once and/or sequentially, it also creates a very chromatic kind of feeling."

Although he comes out of a free-wheeling jazz background and has had practically no contact with formal music—outside of his own researches—Russell has only a limited faith in improvisation.

He once said, "I believe in composed music that perhaps *sounds* improvised but nevertheless is composed." But within the framework of the composed piece, he added, he believes that there should be improvisation.

In this he takes an almost diametrically opposed point of view to that of one of the most highly individual members of the jazz *avant garde*, Cecil Taylor, an academically trained pianist who is very much aware of the European-oriented composers of the twentieth century, particularly Bartok, Stravinsky and Schönberg, and whose approach is completely improvisational. At first, Taylor's classical training was so dominant that it was difficult to discern any real jazz influences in his work. Whitney Balliett has described these early efforts as approximating "what might have happened if a gifted modern classical pianist had sat down at the keyboard and attempted to improvise whole compositions in the combined manners of Debussy, Stravinsky and Bartok. Though this music was worked out against jazz rhythms, it rarely stated the beat, and its largely atonal substance seemed foreign, and even inimical, to jazz."

But Taylor's jazz roots—oddly enough, he seems descended from the Harlem stride pianists through Duke Ellington and Thelonious Monk—eventually began to make themselves felt. Even then, however, his performances were so gnarled and spiky that he could command only a small following and, as a consequence, worked very infrequently.

The preference given to the head over the heart in these intellectually grounded types of jazz performances—a reversal of what had always been supposed to be the norm, the basic appeal of jazz as a music of the emotions—had many effective and effectively placed advocates. But it also had its equally effective detractors. One was Francis Newton of *The New Statesman* who laid what he considered the "sterility" of jazz in the fifties to "a wholly disastrous desire to intellectualize jazz, to make it academically respectable and at ease among the conservatoires, summer schools and *biennales*. Respectability is the death of a music which exists because it is a protest against artistic and social orthodoxy and which operates in a way wholly different from 'straight' music."

Sometimes it was not the music nor the musicians that were complained of but the manner in which they were written about.

"I am distressed by the idea of the amount of pompous, confusing nonsense jazz criticism may produce in this period when jazz musicians are increasingly conscious of the diversity of musical forms," wrote *The Saturday Review's* Wilder Hobson. "Words like modal, polytonal and atonal are fine things to bandy about with a show of authority. They are, of course, no more than indications of certain procedures; they say nothing about the quality of a given piece of music that employs these procedures. But they lend themselves to a bogus air of significance."

86

Aaron Copland, noticing the same phenomenon, remarked that "erudition in jazz often has a phony sound. Often, the ones who sound off are pretentious, as if they have to make something of jazz with fancy explanations.

"Actually," he added, "the jazz field is full of arrangers posing as composers."

SIX

Reacceptance

The postwar years of jazz were not devoted solely to an endless search for something new. This was also a period of discovery and of consolidation. It was a period when what may prove to be an inevitable cycle in jazz was demonstrated making its full sweep. During the decade of the thirties, most of the great jazz musicians of the twenties who still survived fell into obscurity. One notable exception was Louis Armstrong but these were harsh years for such men as Jelly Roll Morton, Johnny Dodds, Jimmy Noone, Kid Ory and others of the earlier period, for they were buried under the avalanche of swing. Their crime was that they were no longer in fashion.

But then, in the forties, these men and their music became acceptable once more although Morton, Noone and Dodds did not live long enough to enjoy the return to favor. And meanwhile, as the forties wore on into the fifties, musicians of the swing era found themselves, in turn, being rejected because they, too, had become unfashionable, thrust aside in favor of exponents of the new, young, postwar jazz styles. As the sixties approached, these temporary pariahs were also being returned from limbo although, inevitably, for some of them the time of waiting had been too long.

It is indicative of the relative youth of jazz that it was not until late in the 1930's that the music acquired a past of sufficient breadth to permit some parts of it to become forgotten—or, shall we say, overlooked. By then, however, the early New Orleans tradition had been neglected for roughly seven or eight years—since the onset of the Depression—while big swing bands had dominated the scene. Among the few memories of early jazz that were kept alive were the Dixieland-cum-swing efforts of Bob Crosby's band and Eddie Condon's coterie at Nick's in Greenwich Village.

Then in 1937 four pioneer researchers and writers on jazz—Frederic Ramsey, Jr., Charles Edward Smith, William Russell and Stephen W. Smith—began laying plans for the first American book on jazz, *Jazzmen,* published two years later. In the course of gathering material, Russell learned from Louis Armstrong that he had met one of the earliest New Orleans cornetists, Bunk Johnson, the year before in New Iberia, Louisiana. Johnson had played with the legendary Buddy Bolden at the end of the nineteenth century in what is often considered the first real jazz band. He had continued to play with steadily diminishing financial success until, at a dance in Kansas in 1931, a fight broke out in which the leader of his band was killed and Johnson's cornet was smashed. He had retired then in disgust and settled near New Iberia, a town about 130 miles west of New Orleans where he worked in the rice fields and drove a truck.

Armed with Armstrong's tip, Russell sent a letter to Johnson in care of the postmaster at New Iberia and was soon carrying on an extensive and fruitful correspondence with the high-spirited veteran who signed his letters "Willie 'Bunk' Johnson." It was fruitful for Russell in the sense that Johnson provided him with a vast amount of detail about early New Orleans jazz and jazz musicians. For Johnson, however, the correspondence meant something else entirely. He did not simply want to discuss the past—he wanted to get into action again.

"What it takes to stomp 'em, I really knows it yet," he wrote to Russell. "I'm an old man in years but not in action and playing."

Much as he might want to "stomp 'em," however, Johnson was faced with two problems: he had no horn and even if he had had one he could scarcely have played it because he had lost all his teeth. As a gesture of appreciation for the help Johnson had given him, Russell and some of his friends raised enough money to get him some store teeth (made by Sidney Bechet's brother, Dr. Leonard Bechet, a New Orleans dentist and onetime trombone player) and a trumpet, personally selected by Louis Armstrong.

While Johnson was breaking in his teeth and his trumpet in the spring of 1940, Heywood Hale Broun, son of the newspaper columnist, Heywood Broun, and a devoted follower of New Orleans jazz, arrived in New Orleans with the intention of recording a group of New Orleans veterans. The recordings that Broun made with trumpeter Kid Rena, two of the most vaunted New Orleans clarinetists—Alphonse Picou and Big Eye Louis Nelson—guitarist Willie Santiago, seventy-year-old Albert Gleny on bass, Rena's brother, Joe, on drums and Jim Robinson, a relatively young trombonist who was a last-minute fill-in, constituted the first overt step in what was to become known as the New Orleans revival. Broun's discs, released on his own Delta label, were inexpertly balanced and rather crudely recorded on portable equipment (this was before the time when tape recording simplified such efforts) but they created a tremendous wave of excitement among a knowledgeable hard core of jazz fans for, in addition to being the first recordings made by New Orleans musicians in many years, they were the first examples of New Orleans marching band music that had ever been recorded.

As Broun's records were put into circulation, word came north from New Orleans that Bunk Johnson was making good use of his new teeth and trumpet. Bunk was really playing again, so well in fact that Russell and Gene Williams, editor of the magazine *Jazz Information,* went to New Orleans in 1942 and recorded him for a small Los Angeles record company, Jazz Man Records. Russell later said that this was the most wonderful music he had ever heard in his life but the records were almost thrown away by an engineer who came across them while he was cleaning out a studio and thought they were a joke.

Johnson was sixty-two years old when he made these initial records. A year later he was invited to San Francisco to appear at the last of a series of lectures on jazz by Rudi Blesh at the Museum of Modern Art.

"I am right proud to be here," white-haired Bunk Johnson told the Museum audience on that April afternoon in 1943, "as I know you all must be to have me."

For them he played blues, he played popular songs such as *Star Dust,* he played spirituals and he played rags (which, he insisted, are "hot as written" in the *Red Back Book of Rags,* the New Orleans musician's standard source of rags, and should be played "as written"). Shortly after this, Johnson appeared at a concert at the Geary Theatre with two more New Orleans veterans who had gone into retirement in California, trombonist Kid Ory and trumpeter Papa Mutt Carey. *Time* magazine devoted a page to the concert and Johnson followed it with a series of Sunday afternoon concerts that became the fashionable weekend activity for San Franciscans.

When Johnson moved on to New York in 1945 where an old catering hall on Second Avenue, the Stuyvesant Casino, was turned into a dance hall for his band, the publicity campaign behind him was in full steam. He was, as Albert McCarthy said, "hailed by purist critics as all that was holy in jazz." At the same time he was the darling of the college set, their greatest discovery since goldfish swallowing. Johnson's autumnal fame continued for the next couple of years. In 1946, when he was sixty-six, his fellow musicians were all in their late forties or fifties (except for one juvenile, thirty-four-year-old pianist Alton Purnell). James Dugan, one of the early reporters on jazz, has recalled the "preposterous scene when these seven gaffers mount the stand."

"It resembles," Dugan wrote, "a blue-ribbon jury going into the box. Dressed in street clothes, the dignified gray-haired men take their places. Bunk, in a tasteful brown tweed and high-top shoes, does some last minute spot welding on his eccentric instrument. His lean left hand with its three gold rings fixes a white handkerchief in place around the pistons. . . . Bunk's skinny elbows rise, he leans stiffly back in his chair and he beats his long foot three times on the stand. The riot starts on the third beat."

But Johnson proved to be a crotchety idol. Despite his association with the past of New Orleans and the fact that he was the focal point of a steadily growing revival of interest in New Orleans jazz, Johnson was not particularly interested in playing the old New Orleans tunes that were expected of him. He wanted to play the current pop hits. And he would rather play prettily than hot. Moreover, he was not overly fond of the musicians in the band that had been assembled for him. As his intractability increased, he was encouraged to go back to New Orleans and rest. It was his last trip home. He died there in 1949.

His band continued, however, under the leadership of its clarinetist, a slight, frail little man named George Lewis, a self-taught musician who was steeped in New Orleans jazz tradition. Under Lewis, the band concentrated on the ensemble style of early New Orleans bands, featuring occasional solos by Lewis, who played with an oddly poignant tone, and Jim Robinson, the robust trombonist who was first heard as a fill-in on Heywood Hale Broun's Kid Rena records in 1940. The Lewis band toured the United States with moderate success through the fifties but had its greatest influence in England where the band's ensemble style and Lewis' quite personal sound on clarinet provided the impetus for what eventually became a flood of "traditional" jazz bands.

Another strand in the traditional jazz revival of the forties centered on Kid Ory, the venerable New Orleans trombonist who had led his own band in New Orleans as early as 1911. Ory had gone into semiretirement on a chicken farm in California in the thirties. Early in the forties, Ory occasionally joined informal sessions with Mutt Carey, pianist Buster Wilson, guitarist Bud Scott and drummer Minor Hall who were working in the Los Angeles area. When Bunk Johnson went to San Francisco in 1943, Ory and Carey went up to join him in his Geary Theatre concert.

At about the same time clarinetist Barney Bigard, still

another New Orleans product, left Duke Ellington after more than a decade as one of the Duke's star sidemen and started his own group in Los Angeles. He induced Ory to return to music on a regular basis as an added attraction with his group. Bigard's combo was not a contributing factor to the traditional jazz revival, aside from its re-activation of Ory, because it worked in a swing style rather than in the traditional New Orleans manner. However, when Orson Welles, responding to the stir of excitement that Bunk Johnson had set up in San Francisco, wanted a New Orleans jazz band organized for his Mercury Theatre radio program in 1944, Ory was included in it along with Mutt Carey, Bud Scott, Buster Wilson, bassist Ed Garland, drummer Zutty Singleton and clarinetist Jimmy Noone.

Popular response to the group was so great that the band continued on the program for three months and then remained together with Ory as leader. From this springboard, Ory became the most consistently successful of the musicians to emerge from the revival. His group, made up largely of well-aged musicians, worked much of the time in Los Angeles and, later, in San Francisco where he had a club of his own. The band also toured Europe several times. Ory continued an active career as a leader into the sixties even though he reached his seventy-fifth birthday on Christmas Day, 1961.

The re-emergence of Johnson and Ory was only one phase of the traditional jazz revival. The other phase was developed contemporaneously with the discovery and re-vitalization of Johnson. It centered on a white trumpet player named Lu Watters. Johnson and Ory and the men who usually played with them were carrying on a musical tradition that was native to them. Watters, on the other

94

hand, had no background either in New Orleans or as a jazz musician. He was a big band sideman in the middle thirties. Unlike the New Orleans veterans who simply cleared the cobwebs from their memories to get material, Watters had to go researching for his tunes.

He and a few like-minded musician friends who were tired of the stereotyped arrangements of the big swing bands on one hand, and the extreme looseness of jam sessions which amounted to a series of long solos on the other, began getting together in the fall of 1939 for after-hours sessions at the Big Bear Tavern in the Berkeley hills outside San Francisco. Here they tried to play in the almost forgotten styles of King Oliver's Creole Jazz Band and Jelly Roll Morton's Red Hot Peppers, digging out the rags, stomp and blues that these and other New Orleans-rooted groups had once played.

The next summer Watters organized the Yerba Buena Jazz Band (Yerba Buena was an early name for San Francisco), following the instrumentation of King Oliver's Creole Jazz Band by using two cornets—Watters and Bob Scobey. Several sessions by the band at the Dawn Club behind San Francisco's Palace Hotel were so successful that the Yerba Buenans were soon playing there four nights a week. The band created such a stir in San Francisco that a record company, Jazz Man Records, was established for the sole purpose of recording it (this same company later made the first records by Bunk Johnson).

One night in 1941 the band invited Papa Mutt Carey to come up from Los Angeles to hear them play.

"When Mutt heard the music," trombonist Turk Murphy later recalled, "he got a look on his face as though he'd seen a ghost. We asked him to sit in and he sort of hesitated. Nobody in the audience knew he was the great

Mutt Carey—I doubt if most of these kids had ever heard of him. We played *Dippermouth Blues* and he took the old traditional cornet chorus. When he finished the people went nuts for twenty minutes. I looked at Mutt—and there he stood with the tears streaming down his face. Then he played and played and played all night long."

Although the band's detractors accused them of being slavish copyists, Watters and his men tried to maintain the essential atmosphere of group improvisation. When the band was learning one of the old tunes, according to clarinetist Bob Helm, it would first be scored and skeletonized for the band to learn it. Then, after a short time had been devoted to getting the tune down, the skeletonized arrangement was taken away and the men in the band were on their own. One piece that the musicians made use of to keep themselves on their improvisational toes was *Terrible Blues,* played in seven flats.

The band was broken up during the war when most of its members went into service, but Watters reorganized in 1946, first at the Dawn Club and later at Hambone Kelly's club, owned co-operatively by members of the band. By 1949, however, the original group began to drift apart. Trombonist Turk Murphy left to form his own group which continued to carry on much of the basic Watters musical repertoire, adding to it barroom ballads, rounders' tunes, riverboat songs and gambling songs which fitted in with Murphy's rough-hewn style as a vocalist. The next year, 1950, Scobey also went out on his own, at first working in the Watters tradition but eventually dwindling down to very commercial Dixieland performances. Watters continued until the first of January, 1951. Then he closed Hambone Kelly's, gave up music and became a chef.

By then the revival had largely run its course in the

United States. In the fifties it leaped the Atlantic to England and France but the main vestige of it in the States during that decade was in the little Dixieland bands—a divergent offshoot of the basic revival—that found increasing commercial favor, their playing growing more and more trite and stereotyped as their audiences widened. In retrospect, the fact that the revival had centered on San Francisco has provided food for thought on the way in which interest in jazz spreads.

"The significance of the New Orleans 'revival,'" Philip F. Elwood pointed out in a history of San Francisco jazz in *Metronome,* "is that it emerged from an area where jazz creativity and interest had been almost nonexistent; an area which had not shown any enthusiasm for up-to-date jazz as had the cities of the East. It is not without significance that the same sort of enthusiasm for traditional jazz which was once associated with San Francisco is now [1961] notably present in other areas of the world such as England whose past also included many years of musical stagnation and isolation from the more progressive elements."

In New Orleans itself, the New Orleans revival meant relatively little at the time. It stimulated the development of Dixieland bands, mostly made up of white musicians, who were soon catering primarily to the limited tastes of the tourists who flooded through Bourbon Street in search of strip joints. Not until almost fifteen years later did the musicians who were the inheritors of the basic New Orleans tradition begin to receive a little attention (aside from those who toured with George Lewis' band). In 1961 Riverside Records brought some of these musicians to the attention of a wide public through a series of recordings. At the same time, through the effort of a New

97

Orlean jazz enthusiast, Grayson Mills, some traditional New Cleans bands could be heard six nights a week at Preservtion Hall, a onetime art gallery that had seats and benche for thirty people. Admission was by contribution to kitty. There was no food or drink; no dancing—just lisning. And in November, 1961, the New Orleans Jazz Clb opened the New Orleans Jazz Museum to display sun memorabilia as a soprano saxophone played by Sidney echet, a bass drum that belonged to the legendary Papa Line, displays on Storyville and Tom Brown's band a well as devices for listening to half-hour programs o New Orleans recordings.

The ind of Dixieland that infested New Orleans in the fiftie was no different from the bastardization of this once brint and flavorsome music that spread all across the United ates in this decade. It was, as John Norris wrote in the Cnadian magazine, *Coda,* "the corniest and most terrible sunding noise masquerading under the name of jazz." Orinally, the rise of the Dixieland tide had been a good-naured offshoot of the New Orleans revival. It received s greatest stimulation when a group of Walt Disney crtoonists, playing for their own amusement, formed aand called the Hugajeedy Eight. In 1948 they acquired ome firemen's uniforms and began playing weekend ngagements as the Firehouse Five Plus Two. It was a rolcking, high-spirited group which made up for any instrmental limitations by its exuberant good nature, a qulity they projected so well that they soon found themselv playing on television and records and acquiring a nationa audience.

The inrest in Dixieland might have rested right there —in good-atured amateurism—if high fidelity and a man named Siqey Frey had not come along. In 1956 Frey, who was producing records aimed at the newly developing army of high fidelity addicts, had his ear cocked for a group with what he thought of as "that happy little brass band sound." He found this sound in, of all places, the chromium glitter of Las Vegas emanating from the Dukes of Dixieland, a family band from New Orleans built around two brothers, Frank and Freddie Assunto, a trumpeter and a trombonist, and their father, Jac, who doubled between banjo and trombone.

The Dukes' first LP recording for Frey, emblazoned with the compelling come-on line, "You've Got to Hear It to Believe It!", had, to quote Frey's description, the "warmth, intimacy, brilliance, clarity, separation, dynamic range and frequency response" that owners of high fidelity equipment wanted in a demonstration record. Hi-fi bugs welcomed this change from what was then the standard fare on ultra-high-fidelity discs—thunderstorms, train sounds and theatre organs. In the first three months that the record was on the market, they scooped up 20,000 copies. More significantly, whenever they showed off their equipment for friends, the Dukes' record was usually brought out and the listeners were apt to be as impressed by the lively beat of the Dukes' music as they were by the miracles of high fidelity. In the following four years, the Dukes of Dixieland made ten more LPs for Frey that sold more than a million and a half copies, and the group became one of the highest paid, most solidly booked musical acts in the country.

Between the faddistic impetus given to Dixieland by the popularity of the Dukes of Dixieland and the possibility this suggested to other groups for duplicating in some measure their commercial success, Dixieland was suddenly everywhere, played in most cases with deadeningly repetitive banality for audiences whose standards of judg-

99

ment were either nonexistent or, more frequently, warped. A Dixie group that played at the annual dance of a country club near New York made such a tremendous hit that they were immediately booked for the same dance the following year. But on its second appearance there were complaints that the band was not as good as it had been the year before.

"The difference," one member of the band explained afterwards, "was that the trombonist was drunk the first time and spread clams all over the place. The second year he was sober and played what he was supposed to."

During the same period in which traditional jazz was enjoying its revival—the late forties—the big bands that had driven it underground in the thirties were going into a decline themselves. A great many factors went into the withering away of the big bands. In part, it was a two-pronged economic matter. Sidemen, even relatively inexperienced sidemen, had become so accustomed to high salaries during the lush war years that the expense of maintaining a big band rose out of all proportion to its potential income. At the same time, dancing, which had always been the *raison d'être* for a big band, was diminishing, pushed aside by the imposition of a war-inspired tax that applied when dancing was permitted. To keep down the cost of an evening out, many places that had once featured dancing filled the dance floor with additional tables, thereby eliminating the tax and also squeezing in a few extra patrons.

As jazz changed from a dancing music to a listening music, there was less and less demand for large bands. Small groups could provide satisfaction for listeners. Furthermore, many musicians were finding that small groups provided them with a more challenging and interesting setting than the stereotyped arrangements they were faced

RCA Victor Records: Shaw Artists Corporation

SONNY ROLLINS

Charles Stewart

JIMMY GIUFFRE

STAN KENTON

James J. Kriegsmann: Monte Kay

THE MODERN JAZZ QUARTET
(seated, left to right): PERCY HEATH, MILT JACKSON
(standing, left to right): CONNIE KAY, JOHN LEWIS

with in a big band, so that it became more and more difficult for big bands to recruit good musicians.

Woody Herman, who had his most successful bands in
the twilight of the big band era, saw the seeds of the big
bands' downfall being planted during the war years.
"At that time bands weren't really trying," Herman has
said. "They were just watching the loot roll in and thinking about the next army camp they'd play."

Herman led his pace-setting band, the exuberant power-
house known as the First Herd, from 1944 to 1946. Because
of his wife's illness, he broke up the band then and retired
to California to be with her for the better part of a year.
But by the end of 1947 he was itching to be back in front
of a band and he introduced his Second Herd at the Pal-
ladium in Los Angeles in the last week of December, 1947.
This was the band that familiarized the saxophone voicing
identified as the Four Brothers sound. After two years, however, Herman gave up this band.

"So many of the great musicians of today have suddenly
become so ultra-modern," he said at that time, in explaining the decline of big bands in general, "that even they
themselves don't understand what they are playing. The
spirit of jazz is abandon but when you present it as too
grimly serious it loses its naturalness."

Herman continued to be active all through the fifties,
sometimes leading a big band, at other times heading a
combo, all of them respectably professional groups but
none that played with the gleaming spirit of his best bands
of the forties.

Benny Goodman, the erstwhile King of Swing in the
thirties, tried to grapple unsuccessfully with bop after the
war and finally gave up his band in 1950. Since then he has
spent a great deal of time in retirement, forming groups

for special occasions from time to time but always depending on the nostalgic appeal of the arrangements of his successful years.

The lithe, easy attack that had distinguished Count Basie's band when it first appeared in the middle thirties began to lose its fluidity during the war years as he lost original sidemen to the services. And after the war the Basie band became almost a caricature of its earlier self. By 1950, Basie, like Goodman and Herman, had given up his big band. For two years he led a seven-piece group and then, in 1952, launched a new big band that, after a shakedown period of a couple of years, achieved a level of proficiency that won it a faithful following. But this was a proficient band whereas the old Basie band had been an exciting one. Reviewing the band in 1960, Jack Cooke wrote in *Jazz Monthly,* "The Basie band of today is often referred to as a machine and the comparison is not inapt. The band can be relied upon to produce a series of well-drilled performances which, though often technically involved and superficially exciting, are basically and essentially unambitious."

The band, Cooke declared, was "an almost characterless arranger's paradise. The great fault of the band is the complete absence of any guiding force."

This lack of character or individuality not only helped to spur the loss of interest in big bands but plagued almost every effort to stir up new interest in them in the fifties. Marshall Brown, an educator who organized several big bands made up of youngsters, including the International Youth Band that appeared at the Newport Jazz Festival in 1958, put his finger on a key problem when he said that "today's top arrangers and composers are not arranging or composing—they are merely manipulating clichés."

"There has never been a fifteen-to-twenty-year period in jazz when less growth took place," Brown declared. "We are living in the era of the interchangeable arranger."

One arranger who remained adamantly uninterchangeable was Duke Ellington, who kept his big band going even when every other leader of stature had either abandoned his band or had gone on a part-time basis. And even Ellington went into an eclipse during the first half of the fifties until a marathon, audience-rousing performance of *Crescendo and Diminuendo in Blue* at Newport in 1956 served to focus attention once more on the tremendously inventive drive that has always been characteristic of Ellington's bands.

More than any other leader, Ellington has a reason for maintaining his band no matter how lean the times may become. Ellington's primary instrument, it has often been said, is his orchestra. But more than that, it is also his score paper, as it is one of the essential requirements for his work as a composer.

"I have a fear of writing something and not being able to hear it right away," Ellington told Nat Hentoff. "That's the worst thing that can happen to any artist. In fact, if the band hadn't always been there for me to try my pieces on, I doubt if I'd have gotten nearly as much writing done as I have. This business of just being a composer, in any case, isn't easy. Look at the hundreds of good composers who come out of the conservatories each year, write hundreds of symphonies and never hear them played. No, I prefer being sure my music will be played, will be heard, and the best insurance is having one's own band around all the time to play it."

Aside from Ellington, the only other leader who kept a big band going consistently from the war years on was

Lionel Hampton. But although Hampton's band was the incubator for an amazing number of important musicians who began to make themselves felt n the fifties, it based its appeal not on its jazz qualifications but on its approximation of the leaden, monotonous attack of rock 'n' roll.

A natural corollary to the end of the big band era was the fate of the musicians who had spent most of their careers in these bands. Like the traditional jazz musicians in the thirties, the musician who could once make a big band swing found himself passed over, dismissed as out-of-date when new forms of jazz took over the spotlight in the fifties. For those who were sufficiently facile to change their styles, the popularity of Dixieland proved to be one means of surviving within music. Count Basie's trumpet star, Buck Clayton, made this adaptation. Others—Hilton Jefferson, the suave altoist of Fletcher Henderson's band, trombonist Claude Jones who had played with Cab Calloway and Duke Ellington—took what musicians often refer to as "civilian" jobs. Rex Stewart, Ellington's cornet star of the thirties, tried both a "civilian" job and Dixieland in the fifties. Some were satisfied to settle into a small but relatively secure nook, as Buddy Tate, once one of Basie's great tenor saxophonists, managed to do at the Celebrity Club in Harlem where he led a band on weekends from 1951 on.

As the fifties wore on, several writers on jazz expressed concern at the waste of talent that the sectarianism of the jazz world was causing through the lack of opportunity offered to these still talented musicians. One of their most spirited champions, Stanley Dance, an English critic, reached the conclusion that the root of the trouble was semantic. These musicians could not attract attention, Dance reasoned, because they were unlabeled and anonymous in a world of labels. Other jazzmen might be identified as Dixieland musicians, New Orleans musicians or bop musicians—each category calling to mind a certain style and certain proponents of that style. But nobody ever thought of these refugees from big bands, as Dance saw it, because they bore no label that would stimulate thoughts of them. To remedy this, he suggested that they be declared "mainstream" musicians. Whether he was correct in his analysis or whether it was because he backed up this suggestion by producing several recordings featuring "mainstream" musicians—Dickie Wells, Buddy Tate, Earl Hines, Buck Clayton, Budd Johnson and others—as well as writing a steady stream of articles about these men, the fact is that by the end of the fifties more and more of these neglected musicians were being heard on records and some were actually working in clubs.

Another boon for the "mainstreamer," if he happened to be a trumpet player, was the discovery by Jonah Jones of what proved to be a highly popular form of music that was sufficiently jazz-tinged to be of interest to some jazz followers and sufficiently uncomplicated and rhythmic to interest a much larger audience that liked to think it enjoyed jazz as long as the tunes were recognizable. By putting a mute in his horn, concentrating on the better known show tunes and playing over a shuffle rhythm, Jones established a style that not only gave him long overdue financial rewards after a lengthy career in jazz but created such a demand for this type of music that many other trumpeters of his ilk—Erskine Hawkins, Cootie Williams, Louis Metcalf, Red Allen, Roy Eldridge—were able to share in it. In general, this resulted in a dilution of the trumpeter's normal playing style. However, Martin Williams, a frequently caustic critic when any signs of pandering to those not versed in jazz are apparent, found pleasure in Red Allen's playing at such places as The Embers in New York and the Palmer House in Chicago. Once a potent and lyrical trumpeter, Allen in the postwar years had been given to loud, fast, raucous and often tasteless performances.

"These flashy pieces do rouse certain audiences on occasion," Williams conceded, "but they seem to me to show the least interesting and inventive side of Allen's talent." In such spots as The Embers and the Palmer House, he noted approvingly, "there can be few up-tempo grandstanders."

There were a few—possibly three or four—musicians of the big band era who managed to maintain their footing even in the darkest days for "mainstreamers." Significantly, these were musicians who had the curiosity and the flexibility to be constantly interested in new developments in jazz but who absorbed only as much of these new developments as they wanted without destroying their own inherent approach or pulling themselves up by their jazz roots. Red Norvo, who entered jazz by the back door playing an instrument that no one else had played before him or since —the xylophone—evolved from a silk-bloused vaudeville xylophonist in the twenties to an outstanding swing musician in the thirties, an associate of bop men in the forties and an enlarging influence on West Coast jazz in the fifties, all without radically changing the way he played. He managed to stay current in changing circumstances by maintaining a constant sense of discovery. In the fifties, when he was studying composition with Dr. Wesley La Violette, he was stimulated by the new resources he found at his command.

"This writing's like opened up a whole new thing for me," he exclaimed. "I used to get ideas but couldn't develop them. Now I can develop the thematic thing. Now I know *why* I do what I used to do instinctively. I'm like a new man, you might say."

Coleman Hawkins, too, had the ability constantly to be a new man. Although Hawkins' influence on tenor saxophone could not match that of Lester Young in the forties, he remained adamantly himself. Hawkins, however, has never stopped evolving. Year by year, from the time when he first outlined a definitive tenor saxophone style with Fletcher Henderson's band in the middle twenties, Hawkins' playing has gone through subtle refinements, a process that has never stopped.

"I always play the way I feel," Hawkins said in 1961. "It can be this sort of a mood or that sort of a mood. But I'm not interested in trying to please other musicians. I just want to please myself . . . and the public, too."

SEVEN

Jazz Around the World

There was a time when the only real audience for jazz was to be found in Europe—primarily in England and France. In the twenties, Americans were scarcely aware of jazz. They knew the word "jazz" of course, and they had great enthusiasm for Paul Whiteman who was accepted as "The King of Jazz," but few had heard of King Oliver or Louis Armstrong or Jelly Roll Morton. English and French jazz enthusiasts, however, were collecting jazz records—real jazz —and discussing them and writing about them. The contrast between the American and overseas audiences was pointed up as late as the early 1930's when John Hammond was commissioned to make jazz recordings in the United States using American musicians (Fletcher Henderson, Benny Goodman, Gene Krupa, Bud Freeman, Bunny Berigan). These recordings were intended for distribution overseas only. The American audience for jazz was so small that it was not considered worth the effort to try to sell the records in the States.

The first book on jazz was written in 1932 by a Belgian, Robert Goffin, *Aux Frontières du Jazz.* The first magazine devoted exclusively to jazz, *Jazz Hot,* was started in France in 1935 (although jazz had been reported on regularly for the previous ten years in an English paper, *The Melody Maker*). The first discographical encyclopedia, *Hot Discography,* published in 1936, was the work of a Frenchman, Charles Delauney. And the following year the first record company completely devoted to jazz, Swing Records, was begun, also in France.

Although much of the interest in jazz on the part of Europeans was based on listening to records, American jazz musicians were being heard there regularly all through the twenties. Sidney Bechet, touring with Will Marion Cook's orchestra, had caught the interested attention of the Swiss conductor, Ernest Ansermet, as early as 1919. The Original Dixieland Jazz Band reached London in 1920 and remained overseas for two years. Noble Sissle's band, which often included Sidney Bechet, played frequently in France in the twenties and thirties. Bechet took a small group to Moscow in 1925. In London in the late twenties, Fred Alizalde's band included Adrian Rollini and Chelsea Qualey, both Americans.

In the thirties, European interest in jazz had grown to such an extent that leading American musicians were able to make triumphal tours. Louis Armstrong went over in 1932 and was greeted in Copenhagen by fans who presented him with a trumpet made of flowers. In London, his concert was attended by King George V. Armstrong ebulliently dedicated one number to the king with, "This one's for you, Rex." The following year Armstrong returned to Europe for a two-year stay. In 1933 Duke Ellington and his band made the trip. By the mid-thirties, a colony of expatriate American jazz musicians had become established in Paris, headed by Coleman Hawkins and Benny Carter.

It was in the thirties, too, that Europe produced the first

non-American jazz musician to win international acclaim
and to have a profound influence on the development of
jazz—Django Reinhardt. Reinhardt was a gypsy guitarist
born in Belgium whose skillful performances with the
Quintet of the Hot Club of France from 1934 to 1939
affected the playing of innumerable young guitarists both
in and out of the United States.

In the forties, the steadily increasing dissemination of
jazz in Europe was brought almost to a halt. In England,
appearances by American jazzmen had been stopped even
earlier—in 1935—as the result of a dispute between the
American and British musicians' unions. The coming of
World War II sent most of the American musicians who
were overseas scurrying home and ruled out the possibility of further foreign tours. More than that, jazz was put
on the proscribed list in the countries that came under Hitler's control, in the Italy of Mussolini, in the territories
controlled by the Soviet Union, and in Japan.

By the same token, however, when the United States got
into the war and American troops began appearing in all
corners of the globe they brought the sound of jazz with
them—on records, in broadcasts and sometimes in the person of the excellent service bands led by Glenn Miller,
Artie Shaw, Sam Donahue and others. To be sure, some
of the jazz-indoctrinated Europeans, on first encountering
American troops, were startled to find that most of them
were more interested in hillbilly music than in jazz. But
still the music was spread and to people fighting oppression
jazz came to have a corollary appeal. It was the music of
freedom. This idea was carried beyond the surface fact that
jazz was American music and American soldiers were serving as liberators. It also led to carefully evolved analogies
dealing with the democratic nature of jazz, the freedom it

permitted the musicians to improvise, the lack of traditional restrictions.

With the end of the war, when Europeans could once
more make contact with jazz, they welcomed it with open
arms. Sweden, which had not been as isolated from jazz developments as the countries of continental Europe, emerged
as the most jazz-conscious and jazz-capable country of the
late forties. Along with Paris, Stockholm became a haven
for a new generation of expatriate American jazzmen.

In 1949 Louis Armstrong began the continuing series of
overseas appearances that earned him recognition as an
ambassador of good will of inestimable value for the United
States. At Stockholm 40,000 fans were on hand to greet him
and the newspaper *Aftonbladet* printed a special eight-page
jazz section in his honor. In Helsinki 7,500 people tried to
squeeze into a hall built for 3,600 to hear him. In Rome
he was met by the Roman New Orleans Jazz Band and
taken home by the band's leader to a spaghetti dinner pre-
pared by his mother, a countess. In Ghana a vast crowd of
100,000 came to listen to his music even though many of
the Ghanians did not have the faintest idea who he was.

American jazz groups were soon penetrating to the far-
thest recesses of the globe. At first these were commercial
ventures but, starting in 1956, they appeared under the
sponsorship of the United States State Department as well.
One of the factors prompting the State Department to begin
sending jazz groups abroad was a front-page story in the
New York *Times* in November, 1955, written from Geneva
by Felix Belair, Jr., in which the official use of jazz as a
propaganda weapon by the United States was urged.

"[Europeans] like to contemplate [jazz], dissect it, take it
apart to see what makes it what it is," Belair pointed out.
"They like to ponder the strength of its individuality and

speculate on the qualities that differentiate it from the folk music of any other country. Somewhere along the line they get curious about the kind of people that first contrived it."

As part of the President's Special International Program, administered by the American National Theatre and Academy, a big band led by Dizzy Gillespie was sent on a tour of countries in the Mediterranean area in the spring of 1956 and later to South America. The same year, Benny Goodman's orchestra toured the Far East. Africa heard Wilbur De Paris' New New Orleans Band in 1957. Dave Brubeck's Quartet covered Poland, Turkey, India, Ceylon, Pakistan, Afghanistan, Iran and Iraq in 1958 while Woody Herman's band traveled through Central and South America and the Caribbean. Jack Teagarden's Sextet, the Herbie Mann Sextet, Red Nichols' Five Pennies and the Charlie Byrd Trio have also been sent out on similar tours.

Possibly the most influential factor in spreading and maintaining interest in jazz all around the world is the nightly radio program broadcast by the Voice of America, *Music U.S.A.*, conducted by Willis Conover. Conover's broadcasts—forty-five minutes of jazz preceded by forty-five minutes of pop music with a fifteen-minute news broadcast in between—are said to have the largest listening audience of any international broadcast despite the fact that they are done entirely in English. There is no way of pinning down the exact size of Conover's audience, but it has been estimated that he is heard each day by thirty million people in eighty countries.

In many parts of the world, listening to Conover has become a social event. Clubs meet regularly to hear his program. A visitor in Yugoslavia, remarking on the scarcity of young people in the streets between 8 P.M. and 10 P.M., was told, "They're listening to Willis." A *Down Beat* correspondent at the World's Fair in Brussels in 1958 found that "every Russian youth I met listened to Willis Conover's nightly show. I got the impression that all young people listen to the show. In Moscow, Leningrad, Kiev, Bucharest and Warsaw, it was the same."

The spread of Conover's following is indicated by the mail that reaches him—from New Guinea ("I have been a regular listener for about five years and look forward to your program every night as about the only bright spot in a very monotonous existence"), from South Africa ("I've heard your voice all over the world, Hong Kong, Far East, etc., and I look forward to your programs"), from Nigeria ("I have so cultivated my interest in the programme that missing it one day is a sort of punishment for me").

Music U.S.A. was launched on January 1, 1955, despite some Congressional objections that a jazz program would simply call attention to the worst side of American culture. At first, the program was beamed only at the jazz-loving Scandinavians, but when letters began coming from other sections of the world ("Can't you broadcast at any time except 3 A.M.?"), its scope was expanded.

The influence of Conover's broadcasts has gone far beyond the mere dissemination of jazz. Musicians in out-of-the-way corners of the world have learned to play jazz by listening to the records he plays. Others have learned to speak English by following the programs (Conover deliberately speaks slowly and very distinctly both because many of his listeners do not understand English readily and to offset the vagaries to which short-wave broadcasting is subject).

When George Wein, producer of the Newport Jazz Festival, returned from a trip through Europe to scout for prospective members of an International Youth Band that played at the Festival in the summer of 1958, he reported that "Willis Conover is the single most important person in American jazz around the world. Behind the Iron Curtain, he sets the musical tastes of many people."

The international nature of jazz in the fifties was made evident by other phenomena in addition to Newport's International Youth Band which brought together musicians from seventeen countries. The sounds of such American bands as Duke Ellington's, Stan Kenton's, Glenn Miller's and Harry James' were constantly reflected in the playing of the regularly organized big bands in Europe—in Kurt Edelhagen's German band (which was made up of musicians from six different nations), in Karel Vlach's Czechoslovakian band, in Ib Glindemann's Danish band, in Ted Heath's English band and in Harry Arnold's Swedish band. In 1960 the Berklee School of Music in Boston was able to form from its students an international jazz septet led by Arif Mardin of Turkey and including a Southern Rhodesian trombonist, an Icelandic alto saxophonist, an American tenor saxophonist, a Hungarian guitarist, an Indian pianist, a Canadian bassist and a Yugoslavian drummer.

In the postwar years, Paris continued to be the most active crossroad of overseas jazz activity, as it had been before the war. Although France was cut off from jazz developments during the war, the interest of French jazz fans never flagged. Charles Delauney, while serving as an underground fighter, continued to work on an updated edition of his pioneering *Hot Discography*. He and other underground fighters who were record collectors made use of their specialized knowledge by communicating with each other in a code made up of the serial numbers of records. The titles of the records, strung together, became a message.

After the liberation, Hot Clubs spread quickly through

France. Amateur jazz bands sprang up, almost all of them following the traditional jazz idiom which was all that the French knew at that point. By 1948, however, modern jazz had made sufficient inroads in French jazz to create a schism between the two leading promoters of jazz in France —Delauney and Hugues Panassie. The two men had been associated in the Hot Club of France. When it developed that Panassie's unwavering taste for traditional jazz could not tolerate Delauney's interest in modern jazz, they went their separate ways. Panassie continued the Hot Club of France while Delauney started the Hot Club of Paris.

In that year Panassie put on a jazz festival in Nice, six years before the first Newport Jazz Festival. In accordance with his views of what legitimately constituted jazz, Panassie invited only traditionalist groups, including Louis Armstrong's. In 1949 Delauney countered with a festival in Paris that drew on both camps—Charlie Parker, Hot Lips Page and Sidney Bechet from the United States, Hazy Osterwald's Swiss Dixieland band, Claude Luter, a French traditionalist clarinetist, and Gosta Torner's all-star Swedes.

Many modernists were among the Americans who settled in Paris on a practically permanent basis. They included Bud Powell and Kenny Clarke as well as such post-traditionalists as Don Byas and Lucky Thompson. France, in the ensuing years, produced many talented musicians in this vein—the pianists Martial Solal and Bernard Peiffer, the tenor saxophonist Barney Wilen. But the tone of French jazz in the fifties was swung toward traditionalism by the awesome presence of Sidney Bechet, the great New Orleans clarinetist and soprano saxophonist who settled in France in 1949.

To the French, Bechet became more than just a great jazz star. He was a great entertainer who was outranked only by Maurice Chevalier. Several of his records sold over half a million copies. His eminence was recognized by the intersection of two streets at the entrance to the Hot Club of France—Rue Bechet and Rue Armstrong.

Bechet's base of operations during his years in France (he died in 1959) was a Left Bank club, the Vieux Colombier. By 1956, besides playing there, he was giving as many as two hundred concerts a year. One of the features of the First European Jazz Festival held at Juan-les-Pins in 1960, a year after Bechet's death, was a parade in neighboring Antibes where the American jazz musician had lived. Two hundred jazz musicians preceded by girls in bikinis paraded through the narrow streets playing Bechet's tune, *Dans les rues d'Antibes,* marching to Sidney Bechet Square where a bronze bust of Bechet was unveiled.

Bechet's tremendous influence in France caused French traditionalists to follow his very personal, lusty manner of playing. As a result, French jazz was scarcely touched by the quite different wave of traditional jazz, patterned on the playing of George Lewis' New Orleans band, that swept much of Europe during the 1950's. The main spawning ground of this attempt to follow an archaic jazz pattern was England. The moving spirit was a trumpeter, Ken Colyer, an admirer of Lewis, who signed on a steamer as a merchant seaman in 1953 in order to get to New Orleans to study his subject at first hand. Colyer spent several weeks there sitting in with Lewis' band (plus a few more weeks in jail for overstaying his visa).

When Colyer returned to England, he took over a band that had been formed several years earlier by a pair of record-collecting musicians, trombonist Chris Barber and clarinetist Monty Sunshine, and shaped it into a semblance of the Lewis band. After a year, Colyer left the group and Barber assumed the leadership with Pat Halcox on trumpet in place of Colyer. Under Barber, Colyer's formula was polished and smoothed out so successfully that the band developed a great following both in Britain and on the continent. Barber went far beyond the basic Lewis repertory and style to include compositions by Duke Ellington and non-New Orleans compositions from the twenties.

In the wake of Barber came other traditional or "trad" bands which simplified the style even more and attempted to add atmosphere to their presentations by dressing in stiff straw hats, fancy vests and other period costumes, something that Barber never resorted to. As time passed and it became apparent that the atmospheric habiliments were more important in drawing an audience than the music that was played, the music of the "trad" bands was reduced to a minimal set of stereotypes that took them beyond all pretense of having anything to do with jazz.

There had been English bands playing in a less limited traditional style before Colyer set his trend in motion. Shortly after the war, George Webb, a pianist, was leading a Dixieland band whose trumpeter was Humphrey Lyttelton, son of an English teacher at Eton and descendant of a much earlier Humphrey Lyttelton who had been hanged, drawn and quartered for his part in the attempt to blow up Parliament. Lyttelton's style was closely patterned on that of Louis Armstrong and, when he formed his own band in 1948, much of his material was drawn from Armstrong's periods with King Oliver and with his Hot Five and Hot Seven. For several years, Lyttelton's was the outstanding traditional jazz band in Britain but in the middle fifties, when Colyer's Lewis-based style was in the ascendant, Lyttelton's interests broadened and he formed a new band that had a swinging style based on the mainstream work of Count Basie and the Harlem jump bands.

Mainstream jazz, with touches of modern, was also represented in Britain in the postwar years by Ted Heath's big band, a powerful, glistening, precision-sharp group, patterned—in execution, at least—on the Air Force band led by Glenn Miller that was stationed in England for a considerable time during the war. Although Heath continued to carry excellent jazz soloists as sidemen, the band solidified its success of the early postwar years by becoming more of a show band and less a jazz band until, in 1953, it was supplanted as *the* English big jazz band by an orchestra organized by Johnny Dankworth. Dankworth, an alto saxophonist, had been in the vanguard of modern jazz in England. He had previously led a septet that had pioneered modern jazz there.

Since then, England has produced a growing number of modern jazz musicians who have won international acceptance, notably Ronnie Ross, a baritone saxophonist of great warmth and fluency, Tubby Hayes, who plays both tenor saxophone and vibraphone, and Don Rendell, a tenor saxophonist whose basic style builds on the Lester Young tradition. One of the most versatile jazz musicians in postwar Britain, Victor Feldman, who plays piano, drums and vibraphone, emigrated to the United States in the fifties, following a trail successfully blazed earlier by two pianists, George Shearing and Marion McPartland.

The desire of Britons to hear American jazz in the flesh in the postwar years continued to be blocked by the feud between the British and American musicians' unions that had started in 1935. Their eagerness reached such a fever pitch that *The Melody Maker,* an English music weekly, once organized a shipload of fans to sail across the Irish

Channel to Dublin to hear a concert by Woody Herman's orchestra. Such extremes of pursuit were finally made unnecessary in 1955 when the unions agreed on a quota system based on a man-for-man exchange.

In the months immediately after the embargo was lifted, English interest in any jazz musician from the United States was overwhelming. And even though English enthusiasm was somewhat tempered after several American groups fell below expectations, the English following for jazz remained so large that George Wein, visiting England in 1959 with his touring Newport Jazz Festival package, proclaimed London "the jazz capital of the world."

"In what other city could the same concert play eight shows and pack every house?" Wein asked in substantiating his declaration. "Not in New York!"

Besides such outpourings for jazz concerts, Britain supports a Jazz Book Club whose members receive a book on some aspect of jazz every other month, and an annual Riverboat Shuffle every summer on the Thames, an affair at which boats loaded with jazz bands, jazz fans and beer go cruising down the river.

One of the wonders of the postwar jazz world has been the rise to a dominant position of Sweden, a country that could scarcely have been found on the jazz map before 1946. The first indication Americans had of Sweden's jazz potential occurred in the late forties when the Swedish clarinetist, Ake (Stan) Hasselgard, came to the United States. Hasselgard was so good that it seemed that he might challenge Benny Goodman's long reign on that instrument. In fact, Goodman hired him, and the young Swedish jazzman was in the unique position of being the first sideman clarinetist that Goodman had ever featured. Hasselgard's career was cut short when he was killed in an automobile accident in 1948, but it was soon apparent that there was a lot more jazz where he had come from.

The Swedes first became strongly aware of jazz during the swing era in the thirties. As a result, Dixieland and traditional jazz never secured much of a grip in Sweden (almost all the traditional jazz bands there are made up of amateurs). For the same reason, an abundance of clarinetists in the Benny Goodman style cropped up. In 1946 American jazz musicians of the modern school began visiting Sweden with Chubby Jackson, Lou Levy, Terry Gibbs, Denzil Best and Dizzy Gillespie's big band in the vanguard. The Swedes took readily to the new jazz styles that these men brought with them. They were, in fact, the first Europeans to go wholeheartedly for modern jazz.

But the Swedes apparently do not believe in abandoning something that is good just because something new and attractive comes along. They clung to their swing foundation even while they embraced bop and produced an amalgam—a swingingly modern style of jazz that is distinctively Swedish.

One of the first stars to emerge within this special context was Arne Domnerus, an alto saxophonist who was leading his own band at the age of seventeen in a restaurant in a small town in Lapland, possibly the most frigid apprenticeship that any potential jazz star has undergone. By 1951 Domnerus was the top altoist in the country, playing with a soft, wistful tone patterned after the style of Lee Konitz. During the fifties his tone hardened, became more cutting as he absorbed some aspects of Charlie Parker's playing and arrived at a musical individuality of his own. One of the members of a small group that Domnerus organized in 1951 was Lars Gullin, a baritone saxophonist who, in 1954, became the first non-American to win a first place in the annual polls conducted by *Down Beat* magazine. At that time he was strongly influenced by Gerry Mulligan, whose quartet recordings had only been available for a couple of years, but later he evolved a smoother, more flexible sound that showed the influence of Stan Getz's tenor saxophone playing.

International reputations have also been won by several other Swedish jazzmen, all modernists—trombonist Ake Persson, chosen by Quincy Jones for the big band he organized at the end of 1959; Bengt Hallberg, a pianist who has assimilated ideas from Art Tatum and Bud Powell; Carl-Henrik Norin, whose work on tenor saxophone has developed from the big-voiced guttiness of Charlie Ventura in the early fifties to a more flowingly Getz-based manner late in the decade; and Gosta Theselius, a pianist who is probably the most successful big band arranger outside the United States.

Theselius does his writing for Harry Arnold's orchestra, a band that can be ranked with the best of American big bands. Arnold uses the cream of Swedish jazz musicians and, since Sweden has more top-flight jazzmen than any other country outside the United States, he has an almost unmatchable personnel. The band is primarily a studio group, playing on Stockholm radio, but it has given concerts abroad in Denmark, Finland and Norway.

Three of the men who work regularly with Arnold—Andreas Skjold, trombone, Bjarne Nerem, tenor saxophone, and drummer Egil Johanssen—are Norwegians who moved to Sweden to find an outlet for their playing. Norway has not developed a jazz interest in any way comparable to Sweden's although there is a Norwegian Jazz Federation made up of almost two dozen jazz clubs which meet regularly.

121

In Denmark the presence of Stan Getz for two years—1959–1961—gave Danish jazz a focus that it had lacked before. Prior to Getz's arrival, the best known Danish jazzman was Svend Asmussen, a violinist who is a product of the swing era. Asmussen is one of the more skillful improvisers on the violin, but as a rule this talent is hidden behind his façade as an entertainer. Getz's extended stay in Denmark gave a shot in the arm to a big, Kenton-styled Danish band led by Ib Glindemann, for Getz frequently played with the band as a guest soloist. One of the problems facing the Danish jazz musician is illustrated in the careers of Max Bruel, a baritone saxophonist, and Jorgen Ryg, a trumpeter, both of whom are capable modern jazz musicians. The economic opportunities in Danish jazz are so limited that both men must earn their livings in other professions (Bruel as an architect, Ryg as an actor) and, as a consequence, they have not been able to develop their jazz talents to the extent that they otherwise might have. One of the very few commercially successful Danish groups is Papa Bue's Vikings, a "trad" band that has been riding the crest of the "trad" fad in recent years.

In the Low Countries, jazz musicians tend to migrate toward Paris although the Netherlands has managed to maintain a relatively independent jazz tradition. Dutch jazz got its real start in the middle thirties when Coleman Hawkins and Benny Carter were touring the northern fringes of the continent. The first Dutch group of note, the Dutch Swing College Band, was formed in 1935. This traditionalist group was scattered by the war, but it was reorganized in 1948 and has become one of the best traditional jazz groups on the continent. Dutch jazz has its modern side, too, but its modernists—who include trumpeter-saxophonist Jerry van Rooyan, alto saxophonist Tony

Vos and baritone saxophonist Herman Schoonderwalt— have not yet reached the level of international distinction achieved by musicians in several other countries.

Belgium has produced a number of outstanding jazz-men, but Paris and the United States have beckoned all of them. It was from Belgium that the first non-American jazz star came—Django Reinhardt, who won his fame in Paris. Jean Thielmans, a guitarist and harmonica player, toured the United States through most of the fifties with George Shearing's group while Bobby Jaspar, a flutist and tenor saxophonist, also spent several years in the States, part of the time as a member of J. J. Johnson's group. Fats Sadi, an enlivening and very rhythmic Belgian vibraphon-ist, has done most of his work in Paris.

Jazz in Germany underwent a decade of steadily increas-ing attrition during the Hitler years. By the end of the war young German musicians had largely lost contact with jazz. They began to pick up the threads by listening to V-Discs and the radio broadcasts intended for American troops, a procedure that produced imitations, often quite competent, of Harry James' trumpet, of Benny Goodman's clarinet or the honking saxophone of Illinois Jacquet.

The horizons of both musicians and listeners in Ger-many were greatly expanded when, in 1948, following the currency reform, records could be bought readily for the first time since the war. Suddenly an accumulation of almost fifteen years of jazz development struck the Germans all at once. Swing, bop and the incipient cool style ar-rived simultaneously and gave the impression of being all of a piece since the steps that led from one to the other were not evident. This situation produced some odd styl-istic mixtures. But with the full spectrum of jazz now spread out before them, German musicians were in a better position to find their way through its mazes than they had been immediately after the war.

During the early fifties there was evidence of a strong Lennie Tristano influence in German jazz, typified in the billowing, linear playing of the Hans Koller Quintet and that of an offshoot quintet led by Jutta Hipp, who had been Koller's pianist before she formed her own group. At the same time Kurt Edelhagen developed a big band that derived many of its ideas from Stan Kenton, Tommy Dorsey and Woody Herman, dressing them in the same glistening sheen that was characteristic of Ted Heath's big English band.

By the mid-fifties Germany had developed two jazz musicians who were considered good enough to take a chance with their talent in the United States. One was the pianist Jutta Hipp who began playing in the American zone of Germany in 1946 when she was twenty-one. At first her style was patterned on that of Fats Waller and Teddy Wilson. In 1951, when she had absorbed some of the characteristics of Bud Powell and Lennie Tristano, an American soldier stationed in Munich sent a tape of one of her performances to Leonard Feather, the American jazz authority. A few years later, when Feather was in Germany, he was sufficiently impressed with her work to encourage her to try her luck in the States. She crossed the Atlantic in 1955, bringing with her a style that was once more in the process of change, this time leaving Powell and Tristano behind to take up Horace Silver. In the course of this change of direction, her playing lost much of the individuality that it had had in Germany and after a couple of disappointing years in New York she drifted out of jazz.

The second German to venture to the United States, Rolf Kuehn (the name was simplified to Kuhn in the

States), was a clarinetist who was introduced to jazz by Miss Hipp in 1946 when she played for him a recording of *Hallelujah* by Benny Goodman. Kuhn was so fascinated that he spent six weeks learning to copy all the nuances of Goodman's interpretation of the piece. Kuhn was featured with several big bands in the late forties and early fifties and for five consecutive years—from 1952 to 1956—was voted top man on clarinet in polls conducted among German jazz fans. By then his original Goodman influence had been succeeded by a leaning toward the more modern style of Buddy De Franco. Yet, when he came to the United States in 1956 (again at the suggestion of Leonard Feather), it was his Goodman background that proved most helpful to him because he was hired to play the Benny Goodman solos in a band that toured under Goodman's name but without Goodman himself. Kuhn had a moderate success in the States, but, like Miss Hipp, he was not able to establish a definite musical personality of his own in the highly competitive American jazz scene.

During the fifties German interest in jazz increased steadily. This interest was fed not only by appearances by local groups and by touring American musicians but also through the use of jazz groups on the various German radio networks. The Southwest German Network at Baden-Baden maintained a jazz and dance orchestra that for three years was under the direction of Eddie Sauter who, just prior to going to Germany, had been co-leader of the Sauter-Finegan Orchestra. Radio Cologne featured Kurt Edelhagen's band. At the Hessische Rundfunk in Frankfurt, trombonist Albert Mangelsdorff led a small group while tenor saxophonist Hans Koller had a similar combo in Hamburg. Jazz festivals were being held in Germany in the early fifties and by the end of the decade four annual festivals had been established: professional festivals at Frankfurt, Essen and West Berlin and an amateur festival at Dusseldorf. In 1960, 250 traditional and modern jazz groups competed in the preliminaries for the amateur festival. Thirty bands appeared at the festival and the two winning groups—one traditional, one modern—were given a two-week trip to the United States by an American soft drink company.

Germany's serious concert halls, like those of many other countries (including the United States), initially tried to sidestep jazz. But faced by the growing acceptance of the music, they eventually gave in. The Congress Hall in West Berlin bowed to the inevitable in 1957 when the Modern Jazz Quartet played a concert there, and a few months later Berlin's venerable High School of Music opened its doors to a jazz concert for the first time when the New Jazz Circle of Berlin presented a program.

More than other countries, Germany has proved to be a gathering spot for internationally organized jazz groups. Kurt Edelhagen's band, which has been called "a UN of jazz," is made up of musicians from Italy, England, Belgium, France, Germany, Austria, Switzerland and Indonesia. A highlight of the jazz festival in West Berlin in 1961 was a European all-star band put together by Joachim E. Berendt, head of the jazz department of the Southwest German Radio Network. It included men from Sweden, England, Germany, Turkey, Yugoslavia, France, Spain, Italy, Norway and Denmark, plus a girl vocalist, Monica Zetterlund, from Sweden. Spain's contribution was a blind pianist, Tete Montoliu, the first Spanish jazz musician to acquire any reputation in jazz. Montoliu "received most of the cheers" at the festival, according to a *Variety* correspondent.

"With his technical virtuosity and artistic imagination," the correspondent reported, "he nosed out even such a great pianist as the Franco-Algerian Martial Solal."

One of the aspects of German jazz that has impressed experienced musicians is the attitude of audiences there.

"They listen intently and with curiosity," John Lewis, musical director of the Modern Jazz Quartet, declared after the quartet had appeared in Germany in 1958. "It's the most musical country I've been to—musical in the sense that everybody seems to have had an opportunity to come in contact with music not just as a casual listener but on a planned basis. This gives them a basis to go on in appreciating any kind of music they encounter. They can relate to it.

"We could almost feel their interest across the footlights. They wanted to find out what was so unique about this music, if it could really compete with other art music."

For audiences on the other side of the German border, behind the Iron Curtain, jazz is even more than just a subject of inquisitive interest. When Willis Conover, who broadcasts the Voice of America's jazz programs, visited Warsaw in 1959 he was amazed to find hundreds of fans and several jazz bands waiting to greet him at the airport.

"You must understand," the American cultural attaché told Conover, whose programs are the prime means by which Polish jazz followers can keep up with the music, "that jazz is a religion with the Polish youth, just like their Catholicism. That's what you represent to them."

The importance of Conover's broadcasts to Polish jazz fans can be judged from the fact that at the end of the fifties jazz LPs cost $12 to $24 on the Polish black market. Obviously, few Poles could buy records at these prices so they listened eagerly to the records that Conover played and when Roman Waschko, president of the Polish Jazz Federation, conducted record sessions at the National Philharmonic Hall in Warsaw, he could draw audiences of 1,200 people.

The Poles have been persistent supporters of jazz. Out of the rubble of the Second World War, the first Polish jazz band was formed in 1945 at Lodz. It was called the Mellowmen, a precursor of a later group using the same name that was considered one of the best of the numerous bands springing up in Poland in the fifties. Two years later Poland's first jazz concert was organized by Leopold Tyrman, a newspaperman. But although this seemed an auspicious beginning for a developing Polish jazz tradition, political changes in 1948 sent jazz underground, denounced as "decadent." During the years that followed, so-called "catacomb jazz" was played in Warsaw, Cracow, Poznan and Lodz despite the dangers involved. Jazz even ventured above ground once a year on All Souls Night when musicians throughout Poland traveled to Cracow for an all-night jam session, a tradition that still continues.

With another shift in political direction in 1955, the official stigma was removed from jazz and it emerged from the "catacombs." Jazz clubs were organized in Warsaw and Cracow. *Jazz Mieseicznik Illustrowany,* the only jazz magazine in a Communist country, made its appearance. Tyrman once again launched a series of concerts featuring the Hot-Club Mellowmen, a unique band led by soprano saxophonist Jerzy Matuszkiewicz, which played both traditional jazz somewhat in the style of Sidney Bechet's New Orleans Feetwarmers and modern jazz with touches of Gerry Mulligan.

During the years of its existence in the "catacombs," jazz had come to be a rallying point for political opposition for many Poles. When Tyrman organized a jazz festival at the Baltic seaport of Sopot in 1956, with six Polish bands and groups from Czechoslovakia and England, it had overt tones of political protest.

"The most important thing for our musicians at that first festival," Waschko pointed out, "was that we were allowed to play at all. At our second festival in 1957, the fact that we could play had been established and was taken for granted and the important issue was whether we should play traditional or modern."

The second Sopot festival had a truly international flavor, both traditional and modern, for the participants included the Two-Beat Stompers and Joki Fruend's Quintet from West Germany, a big band from Czechoslovakia led by Gustav Brom, the Riverside Syncopators from Italy, and the veteran New Orleans clarinetist, Albert Nicholas, who, like Sidney Bechet, settled in France early in the fifties.

Lack of funds caused the Sopot festival to be dropped in 1958, but an event of even greater importance to Polish jazz occurred that year—a twelve-day visit by Dave Brubeck's Quartet, the first American jazz group ever heard in Poland and the first group made up of both white and Negro musicians to be seen there. Brubeck's group exerted a strong influence on the immediate direction of Polish jazz—possibly a little too strong, Waschko felt at the time, because in the wake of the quartet's appearances almost every group in Poland began to adopt the Brubeck style.

In neighboring Czechoslovakia, the jazz barometer rose and fell with the changing political winds much as it did in Poland. In the twenties, as Miroslav Juranek has remarked, everybody in Czechoslovakia was talking about jazz without ever hearing it. During the thirties jazz records from England, Germany and the United States began to reach the country and a real American jazz musician, Joe Turner, a pianist whose stride style had been developed in Harlem bands, came to Czechoslovakia and recorded for the Czech record company, Supraphon (this Joe Turner should not be confused with the well-known blues singer of the same name).

Only one Czech jazzman of note developed in this period—Jaroslav Jesek, a versatile musician who led a big band and composed in a variety of idioms.

With the Nazi occupation in 1939, Czech jazz went underground until the end of the war when the inevitable picking up of lost threads by means of American records began. A magazine, *Jazz*, was started and Graeme Bell's Australian Dixieland band, touring Europe, found an especially warm welcome in Czechoslovakia. Karel Vlach formed a big band patterned after Glenn Miller's orchestra that occasionally veered into jazz. A six-piece modern group, Rytmus 48, was playing under the leadership of a fine trumpet player named Dunca Broz by 1948. But in that year the political stock of jazz went down. Jazz was not explicitly banned, but it was divided into two categories— "good" (i.e., official) jazz and "bad" (American) jazz. By the mid-fifties this interlude had passed. American records were once more obtainable, and an increasing number of modern groups appeared, all strongly influenced by American players.

There were big bands led by Karel Krautgartner, a one-time alto saxophonist and arranger for the Karel Vlach band, and by Gustav Brom. Both bands showed the influence of Shorty Rogers' big band arrangements. A five-piece group, Studio 5, was formed from members of Krautgartner's band in 1957 under the leadership of Ludak Hulan, a bassist, and quickly won recognition as the top jazz group in the country. In 1961 Krautgartner's band, augmented by some of Hulan's men, gave a concert at the Rudolfino Auditorium in Prague, the first time that the cultural authorities had permitted jazz in this previously sacrosanct hall. The program included compositions by Bill Holman, Dave Brubeck's *The Duke* and Gil Evans' adaptation of *The Maids of Cadiz*.

A year earlier Czechs had had an opportunity to hear their first American jazz musician in person since Joe Turner's visit in the thirties, when clarinetist Edmond Hall spent several weeks playing concerts in the larger Czech towns, backed by Gustav Brom's band. Because their contacts with American jazz musicians were so rare, Czech musicians had had to rely on their own uncorrected methods of playing jazz. As a result, Hall experienced some difficulties at his first few appearances with Brom's band because Brom's musicians were not accustomed to playing with a man who improvised continually.

In other Iron Curtain countries, jazz has occasionally managed to peep through official restrictions. Hungary is provided with jazz largely by so-called Magno Boys, young Hungarians who own tape recorders and tape uncensored broadcasts from Western sources. There have been reports of a "fabulous" pianist, Juncio Korosi, playing in Bucharest, Romania. And even though Yugoslavia at first followed the Soviet pattern of barring American jazz as "degrading," Tito's break with Stalin created a more relaxed atmosphere in which Vojislav Simic developed a big band that has gone through successive periods of copying Ellington, Harry James, Kenton and Basie and which, in 1960, took first place in the band competition at the First International Jazz Festival in Antibes.

The most striking instance of a Canute futilely trying to hold back the jazz tide has occurred in the Soviet Union. There the hot and cool uncertainty of the Soviet attitude toward jazz has kept the music in a relatively quiescent state until recently.

There have been times when the Soviets took a lenient attitude toward jazz. Sidney Bechet scored a great success when he took a quintet to Moscow in 1925. One of his listeners, Alexander Tsfasman, was so excited by the music that he resigned from the Moscow Conservatory and organized what he hoped would be a jazz orchestra. Tsfasman fared extremely well until, with the First Five Year Plan in 1929, jazz was denounced as "a product of bourgeois degeneration" by the Union of Proletarian Musicians.

After that, the official Soviet view of jazz varied from cold to lukewarm in accordance with its public stance toward the West. During one of the thaws, there was actually a USSR State Jazz Band made up, Richard Hanser reports, of forty-three musicians in evening dress and featuring violins. Andrei Gorin, reputedly the best trumpet player in the Soviet Union, was released from a provincial jail where, according to Hanser, he was "serving a term for insulting a Party official," and ordered to Moscow to join the band. Tsfasman, who was then in disgrace because of his pro-American attitude, was offered a chair as second pianist but indignantly refused it.

The USSR State Jazz Band met its Waterloo at a command performance at the Kremlin one New Year's Eve.

"It was a fiasco," Hanser relates. "The music was not sufficiently hot to please the audience but it was far too jazzy to please Stalin. He turned away and began to eat while the band's vocalist, Nina Donskaya, was singing. That finished Nina. The band lost its 'USSR' designation; the number of musicians was cut; salaries were reduced.

After an unsuccessful tour of Siberia and the Far East, the State Jazz Band was dissolved."

Through Willis Conover's Voice of America broadcasts, however, Russian interest in jazz has been kept stirring despite official denunciations. These denunciations frequently lost their edge because the denouncers (and this is equally true in the United States) were confused about what they were denouncing. The musicians themselves were often just as confused.

"Soviet bands offer mixed programs of swing, jazz, rock 'n' roll, rhumbas and even torch songs (condemned by the party as too 'intime')," the New York *Times'* Moscow correspondent, Max Frankel, wrote in 1957 when the Soviet attitude toward jazz was in a lenient phase. "These offerings are generally lumped under the title of jazz.

"It does not take many hours of listening to the jazz band at the Metropole Hotel or the all-girl ensemble at the Grand here to learn that it does not take much for a piece of music to be characterized as 'jazz.' There is many a trumpeter trumpeting 'jazz' here who could not tell a blue note from a red one. Syncopation is strictly optional. Improvisation is deviation and deviation from the blue as well as the red notes is heresy."

Still there was a growing body of listeners in the USSR who were learning to recognize the real thing when they heard it. A student at the Moscow Music Conservatory told a visiting American in 1959 that practically all the students listened to Conover's broadcasts every night. When Dwike Mitchell and Willie Ruff, two American jazz musicians, toured the USSR as members of the Yale Russian Chorus in 1959 and gave impromptu lecture-demonstrations of jazz at the Tschaikowsky Conservatory of Music in Moscow and again in Leningrad, their performances were greeted with fascinated and enthusiastic attention. After a trip through the USSR in 1961, Roman Waschko, the president of the Polish Jazz Federation, reported that he had found considerable jazz activity in Moscow, Kiev, Lemberg and Leningrad.

By the early sixties the official Russian point of view was switching over to an "If you can't lick 'em, join 'em" attitude. In 1961 Alexander Tsfasman, the premature jazz band leader, was permitted to write in *Izvestia*, "Jazz has firmly entered into our daily life and has become an integral part of our musical culture." This turnabout was given the highest degree of authenticity when it was followed by the inevitable claim of Soviet precedence, issued by Leonid Utysev, a onetime Odessa street singer whose political antennae were so acute that he had been able to lead bands with just the requisite degree of hotness for a quarter of a century.

"What some people now call 'Dixieland' music," Utysev proclaimed, "was played for many years in Odessa, in our Socialist Motherland, before it was called to life in New Orleans."

The final lifting of the curtain on jazz in the USSR came in 1962 when Benny Goodman was invited to bring over an orchestra for a six-week tour.

The constant travels of American jazz musicians, both government-sponsored and private, took jazz far beyond the more well-traveled tourist paths. Africans, who had theoretically contributed the rhythmic base to jazz, heard Wilbur De Paris, Herbie Mann, Tony Scott, Bud Shank and Louis Armstrong. At Leopoldville, where Armstrong played to an audience of ten thousand, he reassured a worried official who thought his performance might not be comprehended.

"A note's a note in any language," Armstrong told him.

In South Africa, John Mehegan, a pianist and teacher, found that even though not much was known about jazz, there were three African musicians in Johannesburg that he described as "magnificent" jazzmen. One of them, an alto saxophonist named Kippy Moeketsi, he described as "one of the greatest jazz musicians in the world today . . . deeply rooted in Charlie Parker but has a quality of his own of melodic sensitivity and melancholy beauty and pathos that comes from the very soul of this African."

American musicians who wandered far afield to the Far East and the Middle East in the fifties were constantly amazed at the knowledge that people in these countries had not only of the major names in jazz but of relatively unheralded sidemen. One tourist who attended a Communist-sponsored dance in Rangoon was startled to find that the music he was dancing to was American jazz. Both Benny Goodman and Jack Teagarden stopped off in Bangkok to jam with King Phumiphon Aduldet of Thailand, a jazz fan of long standing.

One of the most remarkable jazz enclaves on that side of the world is Australia which came briefly to the attention of the jazz world after the Second World War because of successful European tours by Graeme Bell's traditionalist band. Before the war, Bell's was the only jazz band in Australia. Its performances were limited to the Melbourne area because all the members of the band had regular jobs there. The war, however, brought American jazz in the flesh to Australia and resulted in a great postwar surge of interest.

In 1946 an editorial in an Australian publication, *Jazz Notes*, by C. Ian Turner suggested that, since many jazz lovers went to Melbourne for the Christmas holidays, a program of jazz events might be organized there at that time. Turner's suggestion resulted in the first Australian Jazz Convention, a meeting of record collectors and musicians from all over Australia. It appears to have been the forerunner of the jazz festivals that cropped up throughout Europe and the United States in the fifties.

The first Convention, in December, 1946, lasted four days and included jam sessions, informal discussions, record recitals, a night at the Uptown Club where Graeme Bell's band was playing, a public concert with ten bands taking part and a riverboat trip on the Yarra River.

At the 1947 Convention a street parade was added to the program, and in 1948 it was expanded to include an "Original Tunes" competition and the selection of an all-star band which played at one public performance. The Convention continued to be held each year in Melbourne until the Melbourne organizers complained that they were tired of playing host and would prefer to go visiting themselves. Consequently, in 1950 the Convention shifted to Sydney, and in 1951 to Adelaide where a jazz picnic replaced the by-then traditional riverboat trip because there was no river available. The picnic was so successful that it was continued in later years even when a river was handy.

By 1952 the Australian fondness for traditional jazz, which had been thoroughly ingrained by Graeme Bell's band, began to weaken and modern jazz was heard at the Convention for the first time. Two years later at the Ninth Convention (and in the same year in which the first Newport Jazz Festival was held), some of the performances were recorded for the first time. The Australian Jazz Convention has continued as a successful annual affair with a steadily increasing number of bands in attendance and a commensurate increase in the cost levied on each delegate.

The other major bastion of jazz in the Pacific area is Japan, the only country in the world in which the American jazz magazine, *Down Beat,* publishes a local edition. Jazz had made sufficient inroads in Japan before World War II to have stimulated a Hot Club of Japan. But jazz suffered the same fate in Japan during the war as it did in Europe under Hitler. In the postwar years most of Japan's jazz musicians patterned themselves on prewar American favorites. There was Fumio Nanri, "the Louis Armstrong of Japan," who had played with his Hot Peppers before the war. There was Shoji Suzuki, "The Benny Goodman of Japan." There was Sleepy Matsumoto whose tenor saxophone style was a mixture of Coleman Hawkins and Lester Young. One singer, whose real name was Kiyoko Maruyama, went so far down the road of imitation that she called herself Ella Vaughan.

One exception to this tendency has been Toshiko Akiyoshi, a pianist who came to the United States in 1956 to study at the Berklee School of Music in Boston. Her first interest in jazz came right after the war when she heard a Teddy Wilson record. Later, her knowledge increased through hearing V-Discs by Duke Ellington, Count Basie and Gene Krupa. She got her first taste of modern jazz from a radio broadcast of a record by Bud Powell. By 1951, when an American jazz group headed by J. J. Johnson and Oscar Pettiford played at an American officers' club in Tokyo and needed a pianist, Miss Akiyoshi had absorbed the idiom well enough to sit in. Two years later Oscar Peterson, who was in Japan with a Jazz at the Philharmonic troupe, heard her playing in a Tokyo coffee shop and was so impressed that he arranged a recording session for her with an American company. As a result of this disc, she was offered a scholarship by the Berklee School.

The attitude of Japanese jazz fans toward American jazz musicians is one of utter adulation. When the Jazz at the Philharmonic troupe reached Japan in 1953 it was taken on a three-hour ticker-tape parade through the streets of Tokyo. A year earlier when Gene Krupa, Teddy Napoleon and Charlie Ventura toured Japan, Ventura reported that "there was nothing the people wouldn't do for us."

"They'd wait for hours just to get an autograph or take your picture or shake your hand," he said. "We'd get off the stand and waiting for us in the dressing room would be three little baskets of cold towels, three big bottles of beer, three stacks of sandwiches—everything in threes."

A decade later, the Japanese feeling toward American jazz had not diminished a bit. Horace Silver's Quintet got the same overwhelming reception in 1962.

"The people go crazy over jazz in Tokyo," Silver said. "After every show there would always be a line waiting to see you. They want you to autograph shirts, handkerchiefs—anything."

Reflecting on the apparently universal appeal of jazz and the esteem in which American jazz musicians are held wherever they go, pianist Randy Weston sat in New York one fall day in 1960 and disconsolately noted that "jazz is accepted all over the world—except here."

"It's picked up momentum lately," he admitted, "but it's still not accepted as an art form. It's like a Ford car— it's an American product and yet it doesn't get the respect it deserves."

EIGHT

Jazz and the Mass Audience

"The Americans," concert pianist Artur Rubinstein remarked several years ago, "are taking jazz very seriously. There's so much money in it."

This was not a cynical statement but an observation of fact. As long as the American jazz audience was a highly specialized, minor minority group, the money-making promotional apparatus displayed little interest in it. The only time the promoters brushed with jazz was a brief period in the late thirties when jazz blended with popular music for a short time during the swing era. The ultimate effect of this contact with "success" was to return jazz to the backwater that it had occupied previously.

During the 1950's it was again discovered that jazz had a tremendous money-making potential and, with the promotional zeal unleashed by this discovery, the audience for various aspects of jazz was broadened enormously. This expanded audience was indicated by the successes of various traveling jazz concert "packages," by the ubiquitous spread of jazz festivals, by the increase in the number of night clubs specializing in jazz and by the flood of LP recordings that this audience absorbed.

Given these evidences of interest, jazz for the first time was granted serious attention by newspapers and magazines. Papers in New York, San Francisco, Washington and Boston hired specialists to cover jazz. The first syndicated newspaper column on jazz was successfully launched by Ralph J. Gleason. *The Saturday Review*, *The New Yorker* and *Show* covered jazz regularly while, on a different level, articles on jazz became one of the staple items in the formula of those magazines devoted to various expositions of the undraped female form.

Books on jazz appeared in considerable number on each season's publishing lists, among them Leonard Feather's invaluable *Encyclopedia of Jazz*, a learned study by André Hodeir called *Jazz: Its Evolution and Essence*, an informed basic history by Marshall Stearns, *The Story of Jazz*, and a fascinating review and commentary on jazz history in the words of the jazz musicians themselves, *Heah Me Talkin' To You*. There were paperback reissues not only of these books (except for the *Encyclopedia*) but of earlier, pioneering works such as *Jazzmen*, *Mister Jelly Roll* and Barry Ulanov's *A History of Jazz in America*.

In the process, jazz acquired such a cachet that it was widely accepted as one of the normal programming elements on "good music" radio stations, particularly on FM.

Part of the popularity that jazz encountered in the fifties can be attributed to what Paul Desmond, the saxophonist in Dave Brubeck's quartet, characterized as "the indescribable worsening" of popular music which gave listeners a choice between the pounding monotony of rock 'n' roll or the equally deadening monotony of so-called "mood music," a pompously empty manner of treating tunes that might otherwise be expected to be of some interest. Turning from these, many listeners reached for a satisfying substitute and discovered jazz.

By the time the average listener had gone through the process of dismay, search and discovery that led him to jazz, the golden opportunities to be mined in jazz had long since been revealed and were being exploited by a man named Norman Granz who, almost single-handed, changed much of the manner in which jazz was presented to audiences.

Granz was a jazz fan who began staging Monday night jam sessions at the 331 Club in Los Angeles in 1943. Unlike most such sessions, Granz insisted that the musicians not only be paid, but paid above scale. These sessions proved so successful that he added Tuesday night sessions at another club. The following year he put on a series of concerts at a shabby, run-down hall called Music Town. In July, 1944, he ventured into a bastion of classical music, Los Angeles' Philharmonic Auditorium, with a Sunday afternoon jazz concert to raise money for the Sleepy Lagoon Defense Fund, an organization that was attempting to help a group of Mexican boys who had been sent to San Quentin prison as a result of a killing during the wartime "zoot suit riots."

"Kids went wild over screaming high notes . . . produced by Illinois Jacquet from his tenor saxophone," *Down Beat* said in reporting the concert. "Nat (King) Cole did everything but card tricks while playing the piano. . . . For serious jazz lovers the concert's best moment was the veteran Joe Sullivan's solo. . . . Los Angeles newspapers missed the boat completely. Not one carried a line covering the concert."

Within a month Granz was back at the Philharmonic Auditorium with a similar show, this time a strictly commercial venture, which he called Jazz at the Philharmonic. By fall, he was offering Jazz at the Philharmonic shows every month.

Granz's shows were built around the concept of musical

141

challenges. Three or four horn men—saxophonists, trumpeters or trombonists—backed by a rhythm section, would attempt to blow each other off the stage in their solos. When one such group had honked, squealed and blared the audience into an emotional frenzy, it would be replaced by a somewhat similar group which would go through the process all over again. As he expanded his operations to include semi-annual coast-to-coast tours of the United States, Granz's Jazz at the Philharmonic (JATP for short) relied most frequently on such musicians as Roy Eldridge, Illinois Jacquet, Flip Phillips, Oscar Peterson, Ella Fitzgerald, Lester Young and Gene Krupa. Within a few years he was able to pay these musicians $1,000 or more a week for playing four or five concerts.

"My concerts are primarily emotional music," Granz admitted. "I've never yet put on a concert that didn't have to please *me*, musically, first of all. I could put on as cerebral a concert as you like but I'd rather go the emotional route. And do you know, the public's taste reflects mine—the biggest flop I've ever had in my life was the tour I put on with some of the cerebral musicians like Dave Brubeck and Gerry Mulligan.

"Even if it's honking," he added, "it's the best honking. And there's no baloney about it."

Granz has said that his objectives in presenting his concerts were—in order of importance—to improve race relations (all of his contracts have always included a nonsegregation clause, i.e., he will not play to an audience that is segregated in any way), to make money and to present good jazz.

"I would rather sell mediocre jazz to 9,000 people," Granz once remarked, "and sell my pitch on race relations with it than operate in a vacuum."

In 1945 Granz taped one of his concerts and released excerpts from it on a series of records (these, of course, were 78 rpm discs; long-playing records were still three years away). This was the first time that a "live" jazz performance, recorded before an audience, had been put on records. It opened up a tremendously profitable new field to disc companies, particularly after LP recordings made it possible to put almost an hour of music on a single disc.

By 1955, eleven years after his first concert, Granz was reputed to have made a million dollars out of jazz. He was the first jazz millionaire. His JATP tours in the United States made between $500,000 and $600,000 a year. Another $100,000 came from tours overseas to Europe and Japan. He had four record labels—Norgran, Clef, Down Home and Verve—which produced an annual gross of about four million dollars. His record catalogues, with four hundred LP titles, were the biggest in the business and he released twice as many LPs in a year as any other company. The fifteen volumes of his JATP recordings (some volumes were multiple LP sets) were approaching a total sale of one million dollars.

There had been jazz concerts before Granz invaded Philharmonic Auditorium in Los Angeles. Some attempts at jazz were included in the concert by Paul Whiteman at Aeolian Hall in New York in 1924 when Whiteman introduced George Gershwin's *Rhapsody in Blue*. Benny Goodman's orchestra had played at Carnegie Hall in New York in 1938. In 1942 Eddie Condon started a series of jazz concerts at Town Hall in New York. At approximately the same time that Granz was putting on his early JATP concerts, Monte Kay and Mal Braveman attempted the first bop concert in a dance hall on East Thirteenth Street in New York.

But it was Granz who discovered the formula that put the jazz concert into a big money-making category. His pattern of programming was followed by others who were lured into the field by his success, although their presentations rarely ran as smoothly as Granz's did once he had a few years of experience. By the mid-fifties jazz in the concert hall was commonly being handled, as Whitney Balliett noted, as if it were a run-down circus.

"The concert almost always begins late," Balliett wrote in a classic description of these affairs, "and, like any sideshow, is generally conducted by a master of ceremonies who is often that pale descendant of the old circus barker, the disc jockey. Indeed, the music is usually buried in irrelevant words, both spoken and written. In addition to a master of ceremonies, there are frequently *two* printed programs, one free, and one customarily a dollar, which are full of encomiums to performers who may or may not appear but rarely mention what is played—information that, like as not, doesn't come from the stage either. The staging, at best, is informal: the lighting is apt to alternate between an overexposed glare and a mysterious twilight, and the microphones are often placed in such a way that if, say, a big band is performing, its soloists, for all that can be heard of them, appear to be engaging in pantomime."

By 1957 the jazz concert field had burgeoned to such a degree that Dave Brubeck could command $1,500 a night with an unbending minimum of $1,000. Benny Goodman, whose fee ten years earlier had been $200 a night, could ask and get $3,500 against fifty per cent of the gate. But by 1957, too, the type of presentation described by Balliett had begun to wear on the susceptibilities of the jazz audience. Touring jazz packages were beginning to report losses. Even Granz's Jazz at the Philharmonic, a consistently successful package for a dozen years, suddenly found its audiences deserting it. At Symphony Hall in Boston, where JATP had traditionally played to two packed houses, it failed to draw enough people to fill the hall once. In 1961 Granz withdrew completely from the field. He moved to Switzerland, sold his record company (his four labels had been consolidated as Verve Records) and devoted himself to managing Ella Fitzgerald and conducting jazz concert tours in Europe.

As the concert packages hit and passed their monetary peak, a new and apparently even more lucrative type of presentation was on its way up—the summer jazz festival. The start of this phenomenon is generally considered to be the first Newport Jazz Festival, put on in the Rhode Island resort town in July, 1954, by a group headed by Louis and Elaine Lorillard, Newport residents, and George Wein, a jazz impresario from Boston. According to Leonard Feather, an earlier jazz festival was held in Wilkes-Barre, Pennsylvania, in 1951. But there had been even earlier ones which, like most pioneering attempts at jazz appreciation, took place outside the United States.

The first festival-like occasion involving jazz may well have been the original Australian Jazz Convention, held in Melbourne in 1946, at which jazz fans and musicians got together to talk jazz, play records and hold jam sessions. The first jazz festival as the term has come to be used was put on in 1948 by Hugues Panassie at the Hotel Negresco in Nice, France. Louis Armstrong's All Stars, which then included Earl Hines, Jack Teagarden, Sid Catlett and Barney Bigard, played at this affair along with Mezz Mezzrow, Bob Wilber, Baby Dodds, Pops Foster and Lucky Thompson.

Another notable festival was held in Paris the following

year which—with such luminaries as Charlie Parker, Sidney Bechet and Miles Davis present—mingled both the traditional and modern aspects of jazz. (Panassie's festival had been strictly traditional.) These festivals and the Salon du Jazz in Paris in 1953 were gala but relatively modest affairs. And so was the first Newport Jazz Festival in 1954. But the Newport Festival opened the eyes of its sponsors to the possibilities for ever-expanding magnitude that seemed to lie in the jazz festival idea.

That first Newport Festival, held on the grass tennis courts of the Newport Casino, began in unassuming fashion on the evening of July 17, 1954, when Eddie Condon and his gang lit into *Muskrat Ramble*. It continued for two nights, attracting 14,000 persons who heard Stan Kenton as master of ceremonies trace an outline history of jazz (from a script written by Nat Hentoff), illustrated by performances by Bobby Hackett, Pee Wee Russell, Lee Wiley, the Modern Jazz Quartet, Dizzy Gillespie, Lee Konitz, Oscar Peterson, Gerry Mulligan and Ella Fitzgerald. The two-day affair turned in a profit of $25,000.

The following year the festival was moved to Freebody Park, a local football stadium which could hold at one fell swoop all of the people who had attended the entire festival the previous year. It was expanded to three days and showed a profit of $50,000. The next year, 1956, was the festival at which Duke Ellington started people dancing in the aisles as Paul Gonsalves ground through chorus after chorus of *Diminuendo and Crescendo in Blue*. The profit crept up to $53,000.

In 1957 one additional day was tacked onto the festival and, for the first time, its producers ventured outside jazz to add a little more allure to the affair by including the singer and onetime dancer, Eartha Kitt, with three members of the New York City Ballet. The profit leaped to $68,000. The festival of 1958 was again a four-day affair highlighted by a big band recruited from jazz musicians in Europe and Scandinavia and the profit was reported at $100,000. In 1959, when a ballet choreographed by Willy Sandberg of the Stockholm Opera Company to John Lewis's composition, *Fontessa,* was included on the program, the accounting sheets showed another leap in the profit to $150,000.

Although the town of Newport had been reluctant about housing a jazz festival when it was first broached in 1954, as the years rolled by and the money rolled in the local attitude changed radically because the festival's sponsors were not the only ones who profited. The Newport Chamber of Commerce has estimated that as much as a million dollars came into the town in the course of each festival. Although this money was spent primarily in hotels, restaurants, bars and liquor stores, it quickly passed through the town to people who often had no direct connection with the festival. A printer, for instance, said that he could expect to collect bills that had been outstanding for many months right after the festival.

With the lure of money for the promoters and money for the local merchants, jazz festivals began popping up all over the United States and in Canada, too (as an adjunct of the Shakespeare Festival at Stratford, Ontario). For the most part, they followed the pattern that had been developed at Newport in offering an array of big jazz names in a huge outdoor arena. Bigness became one of the primary objectives. In 1959 nine major festivals played to 311,000 people and grossed $975,000. In most cases they were—as Miles Davis remarked—"jazz supermarkets." And they were often promoted with an eye carefully aimed at an audience which knew practically nothing about jazz except that jazz festivals were *the* thing to go to. In New York, the *Daily News,* which sponsored a two-night jazz show at Madison Square Garden each June, carried promotional news stories in which Sarah Vaughan was referred to as "the rock-a-dilly filly with the two-octave range. . . . When she turns on the juice, man, all you can do is glow." Dizzy Gillespie was described as "the Orville Wright of progressive jazz and a brewer of bootleg music called bop and blues."

There were exceptions. A modest affair held at Great South Bay on Long Island in 1957 had a relaxed and unpretentious air that those who had been through several festivals by then found unusually attractive. But even Great South Bay could not resist expansion and when it tried to spread its festival over two weekends the next year it became, in the words of Whitney Balliett, "a desultory, aimless affair that made last year's festival seem a legendary event."

At Monterey, California, a determined effort has been made to tread a middle path between money and music. The festival, inaugurated in 1958, has made a major point of building its program around special events—specially commissioned works (Duke Ellington's *Suite Thursday* was written for Monterey) and specially organized performing groups which not only have been given time to rehearse but have been paid for it. In 1959 John Lewis, musical director and pianist of the Modern Jazz Quartet, became musical director of the festival. The only other festival to be under the musical direction of a widely experienced musician was Great South Bay where Rex Stewart, the onetime Duke Ellington cornetist, was in charge. Monterey's willingness to make progress slowly

WOODY HERMAN

COUNT BASIE

Newport Jazz Festival: Weston Associates, EE

ROY ELDRIDGE *(left)* AND COLEMAN HAWKINS

DIZZY GILLESPIE

rather than aiming at an immediate big killing is apparent in its financial record. In its first year, it lost $1,100. The next year the loss was $11,000. But in its third year, 1960, it showed a profit—$6,700—and the following year this was increased to $12,500.

But even to achieve this, Monterey had to make compromises.

"There is a kind of awful fascination watching the natural growth and gradual popularization of a giant jazz production," Richard Hadlock wrote after the third Monterey Festival, the first one to show a profit. "In its first year Monterey was blessed with a kind of benevolent amateurism, born of genuine concern for musical content, that made the new festival something special. There was a provocative panel discussion with Dizzy Gillespie and Louis Armstrong and the people who attended the musical performances seemed unusually attentive and orderly, at least compared to the rowdy celebrants already infesting other similar affairs. It was as good as those excellent early Newport weekends and nearly as stimulating as that matchless, modest first year at Great South Bay.

"For its second year Monterey, still apparently devoted in many ways to high principles and musical integrity, dropped the panel discussion and replaced local talent with bigger names. . . . This year . . . the press releases hammered unrelentingly at the 'superiority' of Monterey over other festivals. A climate of big business replaced the simple charm and enthusiasm. Monterey made the typical American philosophical blunder . . . of equating 'bigger' with 'better.' "

A crucial year for jazz festivals was 1960. This was when the rowdyism to which Hadlock referred, which had been building steadily at Newport by feeding on the lax enforcement of local liquor laws (in 1959 some Newport liquor stores were still open at five o'clock in the morning to keep the celebrants supplied), and the prospect of what one observer listed as "chicks, drinking all night and sleeping on the beach," finally burst loose in a riot on the third night of what had been planned as a five-day festival. The next day the Newport City Council revoked the festival's license and it closed, sustaining a $110,000 loss.

Other festivals began to take nervous second looks at their customers. At French Lick, Indiana, where *Down Beat* had reported in 1959 that "a few people got slugged on the grounds," the local Sheraton Hotel, sponsor of the festival, hurriedly canceled the 1960 event (contracts with musicians for this festival were promptly picked up by a businessman in Evansville, Indiana, who moved it to Evansville). Rioting suddenly became the apparent norm for jazz festivals. At Beaulieu, England, about a hundred teen-agers knocked down the scaffolding holding lights used for televising the festival there, set a building on fire, destroyed a piano, hurled apples and eggs at the musicians. Even a flare-up at a rock 'n' roll performance in Windsor, Ontario, was carried in the press as a "jazz riot."

An understandable wave of caution swept over the once seemingly endless jazz festival audiences. The well established Randall's Island Festival in New York City lost money in 1960. So did the Quaker City Jazz Festival in Philadelphia, the Los Angeles Jazz Festival in the Hollywood Bowl and a festival in Pittsburgh sponsored by a group called Jazz Horizons, Ltd. One notable exception to this pattern was a jazz festival held in Atlantic City for the first time, during the same weekend that rioting was erupting in Newport. This three-day festival reported a gross of $101,000. Its producer, Sid Bernstein, was invited by mem-

bers of the Newport City Council to replace Wein, Lorillard and Company in presenting a 1961 festival after the
Newport merchants decided there was more to be gained
from having a festival than might be lost in a riot. Bernstein accepted the invitation and took a dreadful financial
drubbing at Newport in 1961—he lost $70,000 and went
into enforced (for financial reasons) semi-retirement from
festival production. The Evansville Festival, after an
initial success in 1960, was a financial failure in 1961. A
festival in Buffalo, New York, that had attracted 14,000
in 1960 drew only 11,000 in 1961.

The mere desire for ever-increasing "bigness" was not
the only problem that plagued jazz festivals; programming
was another. Audiences complained that they kept hearing
the same groups playing the same numbers at festival after
festival.

"Obviously the musicians keep playing it safe," George
Simon commented in the New York *Herald-Tribune*.
" 'Why try something new,' they figure, 'when we know we
can get by with what we've got?' "

From the musicians' viewpoint, it was not necessarily
a matter of playing it safe. It was often a question of being
able to play at all.

"No one gets to prove anything," pianist Oscar Peterson
remarked of jazz festival performances. "One of the nights
we were at Newport, I think we did seven minutes. It's
ridiculous to say you're going to book Basie, Ellington,
Shearing, Garner, Brubeck, Condon and so on to play all
on one night. Everybody's standing around and suddenly
one of the organizers rushes up and says, 'Okay, George
Shearing! You're on! You've got four minutes!' . . . I remember John Lewis of the Modern Jazz Quartet complain-
ing to me that after all the fuss and trouble of getting to

the place, he sat down and found the piano was way out of tune."

The most basic elements of presentation have been notoriously erratic in the huge parks and auditoriums where jazz festivals are customarily held. A reporter for *Variety,* the show business trade paper, summed up the third Randall's Island Jazz Festival in that paper's own unique style, pointing out that although it took in more money than the first two editions of the festival, this third try "drew a ding on showmanship."

"Promoters either haven't learned from previous mistakes or didn't implement acquired know-how into action," he declared. "A thousand nights have passed since the opener yet sound and lighting weren't adequate. . . . Staging was poor and stage waits added a good 40 minutes to programs that broke at 1 and 2 A.M. Routining and talent booked ranged from ordinary to wretched."

With very few exceptions, the concept of a jazz "festival" has consisted simply of an array of prime jazz attractions. Little thought is given to programming and even less to providing any of the special occasions that one might expect of something called a festival. Monterey and, to a lesser extent, Newport have attempted to give some attention to these aspects but the first real effort to produce a jazz festival of both breadth and depth occurred in the spring of 1962 in Washington, D.C., under the sponsorship of the President's Music Committee of the People-to-People Program, a group which maintains and encourages contacts with cultural groups in other countries.

Billed somewhat inaccurately as "The First International Jazz Festival" (Hugues Panassie's jazz festival in Nice in 1948 was at least as international as this 1962 affair), it offered—in addition to the customary line-up of popular jazz groups presented under conditions which were, if anything, even worse than those that normally exist at jazz festivals—a program of jazz in symphonic settings, an evening of jazz ballet, a jazz liturgical service, a program designed to illustrate the influences of jazz on chamber music, a showing of jazz excerpts from films, six specially commissioned new jazz compositions, an exhibition of jazz memorabilia and the unusual sight of a New Orleans brass band parading through the streets of Washington. Although it was not difficult to find fault with much of the music that was played in the course of the festival, it could not be denied that this was the most ambitious effort yet made to make a jazz festival live up to the term "festival."

Since Newport set the stage for the proliferation of jazz festivals in the United States, only two series of festivals have managed to escape critical barbs of some sort. One—the Virginia Beach Jazz Festival, organized by Tom Gwaltney, a clarinetist and vibraphonist—did this by setting modest goals and by resisting any temptation to be lured away from them by an initial success. Started in 1959, the Virginia Beach Festival (held at a shore resort in Virginia) has limited itself to two nights, largely eschewed big names and depended almost as much on local musicians as on those brought in from the outside.

The other festival that escaped criticism was held under circumstances in which complaint would be difficult even if anyone wanted to register one. It was held in the Lorton Reformatory near Washington, D.C. The only ticket of admission was a sentence to the reformatory. This annual affair began in 1956 when the Reverend Carl L. Breitfeller, the prison chaplain, asked Sarah Vaughan to autograph a picture for one of the inmates. While she was signing, Miss

Vaughan volunteered to sing for the prisoners. Since then the inmates of Lorton have heard, among others, Jack Teagarden, Count Basie, Louis Armstrong, Lambert Hendricks and Ross, Art Blakey and the Jazz Messengers, the Oscar Peterson Trio and Duke Ellington and his Orchestra.

The spreading interest in jazz, as evidenced by the huge crowds who could be lured to jazz festivals and by the massive sale of jazz records (estimated at eighty million dollars annually by the end of the fifties), encouraged the use of jazz in other areas in which it was desired to make contact with a broad contemporary audience.

A brief epidemic of reading poetry to jazz started in 1957 when the American poets, Kenneth Rexroth and Lawrence Ferlinghetti, read their poems to the accompaniment of jazz groups at The Cellar in San Francisco. Poetry and jazz soon became a fad in San Francisco and spread up and down the West Coast. Ferlinghetti wrote what is alleged to be the first poem in English written specifically to be read to jazz accompaniment.

Although this was looked on at the time as an unusual combination of arts, it had a long heritage behind it. As Rexroth pointed out, renegade monks were doing the sixteenth century equivalent of it four hundred years ago. Charles Cros, a nineteenth century poet, had read his works to the music of a *bal musette* band. Maxwell Bodenheim, an American poet and novelist, read his poems to jazz in the twenties and Langston Hughes did it in the thirties. Rexroth himself tried it in the twenties with the help of a pianist named Kansas City Frank Melrose.

When the poets tried to bring their new art to the East Coast, it fell on arid ground. In 1958 Rexroth read at the Five Spot in New York, backed by Pepper Adams' group, and, as one observer noted, "He knocked out the poetry fans but he lost the jazz buffs."

154

Jack Kerouac, the beatnik novelist, was booked into the Village Vanguard and lasted only two performances when the management discovered that he was drawing an almost exclusively beatnik trade which spent no money. Another club auditioned six poets privately, selected two of them to declaim for the customers and then canceled them after one performance when one of the musicians ran screaming from the bandstand, shouting, "I can't stand it!"

At the same time jazz began an association with religion that was not received with any more evident warmth but, possibly because of the fact that the music was presented in churches, the reaction was a bit more polite than that to the poets in night clubs. Jazz entered the church through a twentieth century Jazz Mass which was composed by the Reverend Geoffrey Beaumont, the vicar of St. George's Church in Camberwell, London, because, he said, he was "deeply concerned that nothing has been written since the Elizabethans which can properly be called a Folk Mass." Church music now in use, he declared, was utterly foreign to the majority of people.

Dr. Beaumont's mass reached the United States in the following year and received performances in Boston, Massachusetts, Providence, Rhode Island, and Norwalk, Connecticut. Hearing it at Norwalk, Harold C. Schonberg, music critic of the New York *Times,* wrote, "Nothing much is wrong with the score except that it was pretty bad music." This point of view was echoed in blunter terms three years later by Paul Hume, music critic of the Washington *Post,* when he called a jazz liturgical service written by Edgar Summerlin and presented during the First International Jazz Festival in Washington, "bad music, badly written."

Summerlin has become the composer most closely identified with jazz church services. He ventured into the field almost simultaneously with Dr. Beaumont. Summerlin, a clarinetist, was teaching arranging and instrumentation at North Texas State College at Denton, Texas, when he learned that his nine-month-old daughter, Mary Jo, was dying of a congenital heart defect. To help him assuage his grief, the Reverend Bill Slack, assistant pastor of the First Methodist Church in Denton, suggested that Summerlin set a traditional church service to jazz. The result, *Requiem for Mary Jo,* was first performed at Southern Methodist University in Dallas, Texas, later was seen on television on the program *World Wide '60,* and was played in several churches and colleges. Summerlin has also written a musical setting to a modern religious poem, *Let Us Pray,* for the television program, *Look Up and Live,* as well as the jazz liturgy heard in Washington.

"If the church is going to meet the needs of young people," Summerlin has said, "it must recognize the fact that *The Old Rugged Cross* is not a very real part of our contemporary society."

A slightly different approach to jazz in church—one that harks back to the early association between jazz and religious music in and around New Orleans—was attempted in Albuquerque, New Mexico, in 1961 when McKoskey's Dixieland All Stars, a seven-man group made up of businessmen who played jazz as an avocation, performed at a Sunday evening church service that also featured a modern dance group. The band played such pieces as *Shall We Gather by the River, Down by the Riverside* and *When the Saints Go Marching In.*

The service prompted a Baptist minister to write a letter to an Albuquerque newspaper.

"It is hard for me in my wildest imagination to picture Christ dancing or living it up with a jazz band," he asserted. "We consider a jazz band in the church a blasphemy against the name of Christ."

The relationship of jazz and the church fared much better when it was put on a personal basis. Several priests and ministers during the fifties found that an interest in jazz and jazz musicians was a useful part of their work. The respectable association of the ministry and jazz first gained nationwide attention in the United States when the Reverend Alvin Kershaw, appearing as a contestant on the television program, *The $64,000 Question,* chose jazz as his field of expertise and proved to be a highly knowledgeable connoisseur of traditional jazz. One of the leading jazz commentators and proponents in the East was a Paulist priest in Boston, Father Norman O'Connor, a familiar figure at the Newport Jazz Festivals both as master of ceremonies and reporter. He also produced regular series of television and radio programs in Boston.

In New York, Pastor John Gensel of the Church of the Advent was commended by the magazine *Christian Century* in 1961 for "his unique ministry to jazz musicians, many of whom dwell in the upper Broadway neighborhood of his church. . . . Dressed in his clerical garb, Pastor Gensel visits bars, cafés and night clubs, drinking Coca-Cola and ministering to his 'parishioners.' "

Under Pastor Gensel's instigation, a three-day workshop on contemporary jazz was sponsored by the United Lutheran Church in America at a Greenwich Village night club in 1962. It was attended by 106 churchmen.

In California, Father Kennard, a jazz-oriented instructor in philosophy at Loyola University in Los Angeles, has asserted, "To swing is to affirm." To which Professor Wilson Wade, professor of religion at Dartmouth College, has added, "Then let us swing."

Such evidences of acceptance as jazz has received from men of the church are less apparent in the more worldly areas of communication. Both films and television have made very limited use of jazz. A program of jazz films was shown at the First International Jazz Festival in Washington in 1962. These had been collected by Ernest S. Smith, a pioneer in gathering and preserving jazz that has been put on films. His two-hour show ranged from 1929 (Bessie Smith singing *St. Louis Blues*) to 1952 (a reminiscence by Kid Ory, the New Orleans trombonist, made in France). Most of his program was made up of brief episodes snipped from feature films or shorts, most of them incredibly hackneyed in presentation although the music was frequently fascinating.

Before the fifties, Hollywood's only use of jazz was as a brief spot in a full-length film. In the early fifties jazz won a more prominent place in a picture called *New Orleans* (in which Louis Armstrong, Billie Holiday and Woody Herman were seen and heard) and in pictures based on the careers of Benny Goodman, Gene Krupa and Red Nichols. Original material by jazz musicians began to find its way onto film sound-tracks with *The Wild One* in which a score written by Leith Stevens was played by Shorty Rogers and a group of West Coast musicians. Chico Hamilton provided themes and played some of them for *Sweet Smell of Success.*

Elmer Bernstein's widely publicized pseudo-jazz score for the film *The Man with the Golden Arm* did less for jazz in films than for jazz on television, for the ominous style used by Bernstein was quickly adopted as the most suitable background for almost any private eye series on TV (the most successful was Henry Mancini's score for *Peter Gunn*).

A breakthrough for jazz in films seemed to have occurred when Johnny Mandel was commissioned to write the score for *I Want to Live* which was played by a large jazz group conducted by Mandel and by a small group led by Gerry Mulligan. But even though his score was received well, Mandel was given no immediate opportunity to follow through with further scores. Duke Ellington was finally recognized by Hollywood when he was asked to do the score for *The Asphalt Jungle*, followed by *Paris Blues* and *Anatomy of a Murder*.

In general, foreign film producers were more receptive to jazz scores than American producers, taking one step further the consistent pattern of readier acceptance for jazz abroad than at home. John Lewis' first film score was for a French film, *One Never Knows*. Miles Davis and Duke Jordan also supplied scores for French films and Dave Brubeck wrote one for an English film.

Part of Hollywood's problem was that it could not decide what to do about jazz in relation to films. Was jazz *really* popular—in the Hollywood sense of "popular"—or would it be better to dodge any jazz aspects of a film? This dilemma—and a solution—was pointed up in a newspaper advertisement for a highly regarded and beautifully photographed short film built around the Newport Jazz Festival, *Jazz on a Summer's Day*. In the ad, the title of the film was made relatively inconspicuous while the largest and most eye-catching type in the layout was given to two words which the film's publicists had had the good fortune to find conveniently juxtaposed in a review that appeared in *The Saturday Review*: "Embarrassingly Intimate!"

On television, jazz, as has been noted, was used mainly as background for crime shows, a tendency that has not been viewed enthusiastically by some musicians.

"I think it may kill jazz," pianist Dick Marx remarked. "All these crime programs with jazz in the background are setting up in people's minds an association between jazz and crime and slick, cheap women."

Aside from its cops and robbers aspects, jazz has been heard infrequently on television and then only in its simplest, most diluted forms with the apparent intention of offending as few people as possible rather than of actually pleasing anyone. The most persistent sponsor of jazz—or pseudo-jazz—has been a watch company, Timex. A typical Timex program, produced in 1958, had Garry Moore as master of ceremonies, the Dukes of Dixieland, a duet between Louis Armstrong and Jaye P. Morgan, a drum battle between Cozy Cole and Gene Krupa and brief glimpses of George Shearing, Jack Teagarden and Gerry Mulligan.

Ideas for jazz television programs have run into steady sponsor resistance in the United States but this does not mean that sponsors have been deaf to the appeal of jazz. In 1962 Mike Bryan, a guitarist who had once played with Benny Goodman and Artie Shaw, was commissioned to produce a series of jazz television shows for the Goodyear Rubber Company that would be shown in Europe, Africa and Asia—but not in the United States.

Although jazz was all but driven off radio during the fifties by rock 'n' roll, it was beginning to find a growing audience on FM stations in the early sixties. In 1954 the only regularly scheduled program of jazz recordings in New York City was a weekly half hour on a "good music" station, WQXR. By 1962 this program had been expanded to an hour and was only one of many jazz programs that could be heard on almost every FM station in the area.

In Los Angeles an FM station, KNOB, was the first station to attempt total jazz programming, starting in 1957.

It was later joined by KJAZ in San Francisco and WJZZ in Bridgeport, Connecticut. Dave Brubeck served as music director for the latter station but it had to give up its all-jazz policy after a year on the air because of lack of financial support.

The American theatre, as represented on Broadway, has been practically oblivious of jazz. Benny Goodman and Louis Armstrong once appeared in a swing version of *A Midsummer Night's Dream* called *Swingin' the Dream* in 1939 and Sidney Bechet and Bobby Sherwood played the roles of jazz musicians in a play shortly after World War II. The only notable use of jazz in the theatre has been the off-Broadway production of *The Connection,* a play about a group of heroin addicts who are waiting for their "connection" to arrive with the drug.

The score for the New York production was written by pianist Freddie Redd and played onstage by four musicians including Redd and alto saxophonist Jackie McLean, all of whom appeared as characters in the play. When it was produced in Los Angeles, a new score was created by tenor saxophonist Dexter Gordon who, like Redd in New York, also appeared in the play.

Epilogue

The relatively simple, small and comfortable world of jazz that existed before World War II has disappeared forever. No matter what future path jazz may take, it can never return to the blithe innocence of those days. It has grown from what was basically a natural folk music to become, in some of its aspects, an art music that is often extremely self-conscious.

In the process of stretching out, jazz has shown encouraging signs of a maturity that can compensate for its loss of innocence. The provincialism that accompanied the revolt of the younger generation in the forties, when the jazz world split into small, suspicious, self-limiting groups, has been largely dissipated. During the fifties, the inter-relationship of the various elements of jazz was gradually recognized once more. The evidence of this broader viewpoint could be seen in the simultaneous interest in the revitalized position of the blues singer and the return to some measure of acceptance of the "mainstream" musicians while both the explorations of Ornette Coleman and the cross-breeding attempts in the third stream were attracting followers.

In part, this decrease of provincialism in the overall jazz picture can be attributed to the postwar fact that jazz is no longer exclusively an American music and that the non-American jazz musician is no longer the second class jazz citizen that he was before the war. Taken sectionally, provincial attitudes still continue in jazz. But because jazz now has many homes instead of one, there is more opportunity for the various traditions of jazz to find some area that will support them.

In the United States jazz continues to be subject to the whims of a young public whose changing interests produce a constant demand for new approaches. Nat Hentoff took ironic note of this in 1960 during the first flurry of excitement about Ornette Coleman when he remarked, "Coleman may not see his first gray hair before he *does* see from the stand a musician at the bar shake his head, turn to a colleague and say, 'Man, wouldn't you think he'd get *tired* of playing that simple stuff all night long.'"

If the United States still represented the totality of the world of jazz, we might expect to see jazz continue its jittery, heedless leaps from one new sensation to the next. Fortunately, however, the traditions of jazz are now finding, outside of the United States, havens that they can no longer find at home. This point was emphasized by the two groups that provided the "international" aspect for the First International Jazz Festival held in Washington, D.C., in the spring of 1962—Chris Barber's band from England and the Wreckers from Poland.

Both groups, one playing in the traditional jazz vein, the other in a postwar style, were assimilators rather than creators. Before World War II, the role of assimilators was usually carried out by white jazz groups in relation to the music created by Negro musicians. Thus, the white Chicagoans of the late twenties—the groups stemming from the Austin High School Gang—drew on the whole panorama of New Orleans and Chicago jazz that had preceded them. And similarly Benny Goodman, in the thirties, polished up a big band style that had been formulated years earlier by Fletcher Henderson and Don Redman.

By the 1950's this type of assimilation was no longer taking place in the United States. By and large, the older styles were either scorned or burlesqued while the modern styles disappeared into limbo as soon as their day had passed. But over in England Chris Barber was playing styles that ranged from early New Orleans to swing. Barber was doing this not as a purist or as an imitator but as one who found creative inspiration in the whole prewar period of jazz. The Polish group, the Wreckers, had not yet developed to the extent that the Barber band had when it made its appearance in Washington but even then it was apparent that this group, too, was drawing on the field of postwar jazz as a whole, not simply copying individuals or groups.

As long as there are jazz musicians such as these who find such creative inspiration in noncontemporary jazz that they can maintain an audience, jazz may be able to survive the constant craving for newness that it must face in the United States.

The new elements in jazz at the beginning of the sixties appeared to be channeled in two divergent directions. On one hand, there was an increasing interest in escaping from shackles of all kinds—freedom as expressed in the completely unfettered performance. Along with this came an equally determined drive to make jazz a contributory factor to a broader concept of music—in essence, to have jazz absorbed just as jazz itself once absorbed ragtime.

Either approach may result in valuable developments for

music in general. But both approaches are loaded with booby traps. Freedom per se endangers the easy, warm communicativeness that has always been one of the most engaging features of jazz. Jimmy Knepper, a trombonist who has been through the iconoclastic Mingus school, has expressed concern at jazz performances that leave the listener so far up in the air that he has nothing to cling to.

"Jazz some day has to get some form to it," Knepper has said. "Musicians have to think better when they solo. Tatum, Parker and a few others got jazz out of the simple stage and now it's imperative to be a virtuoso. I'd like to hear Mozart or one of those other 'classical' people playing jazz. The king would say to them, 'Play this melody.' So they'd play this impromptu but they had beautiful thoughts—a beginning, a middle and an end. Their music sounds formal now and yet they were improvising, developing themes, turning them upside down."

Form, in itself, can lead to the sublimation of jazz. When form is drawn from non-jazz sources, it has often proved highly constricting. Wilder Hobson noted two facts about a form-filled jazz future.

"The first," he said, "is that in the jazz world today there is much more interest than ever before in general musical theory and procedures (modal writing, polytonality, atonality, etc.). This would seem to suggest an increasing linkage of jazz with the general, international body of musical development. The second obvious fact is that jazz has still produced little or nothing in the way of extended musical structures. The most ramified works of such jazz composers as Duke Ellington and John Lewis are architecturally simple by conventional musical standards. Here there is the suggestion of syncopated worlds to conquer."

One method of conquering these syncopated worlds has

been indicated by Meyer Kupferman, a composer who has demonstrated a talent for writing carefully planned and constructed music that has the potential of skillfully improvised jazz. To have this potential realized, Kupferman's music must be played by a relatively rare type of musician —an exceptional reader with instinctive jazz feeling. Three such musicians—Harvey Estrin, alto saxophone, Dick Romoff, bass, and Herb Harris, a brilliant drummer—have given a fascinating display of the loose, swinging ease that can be drawn from a Kupferman composition in their performances of his *Infinities*.

The most hopeful thing about jazz as it reached the sixties, however, was not that it had achieved the flexibility to move simultaneously into both formality and formlessness. Rather, it was the fact that, as jazz moved out toward these two extremes, it had for the first time a firm anchor to windward represented by those jazz musicians and jazz fans in far-flung areas of the world who play and support the older forms of jazz which are the heritage on which any jazz of the future must grow. The postwar jazz explosion that sent this American music around the world has enabled jazz to achieve a living balance that it never had before—a balance which can prevent jazz from becoming such a thoroughly footloose music that, unaware of its own sources, it could be blown into oblivion by any of the musical adventures that are essential to its further development.

Glossary

After hours session—an informal performance by musicians after their regular working hours.

Bag—"to work out of a bag"—a style of performance or type of music.

Bop—generic term identifying music as played by Charlie Parker, Dizzy Gillespie and those associated with them in the 1940's. Same as be-bop.

Bridge—the middle or variant section of a standard popular song which is constructed in a pattern of AABA, "B" being the bridge. Also known as "channel" or "release."

Bugged—annoyed.

Cats—people, usually male.

Chick—girl.

Clams—mistakes in a musical performance.

Cool jazz—a subdued, often introverted manner of playing whose restraint was the opposite of the open emotionality of "hot" jazz.

Fluff—mistake in a musical performance. Same as "clam."

Funk—earthiness.

Hard bop—a revival in the 1950's of the bop style of the 1940's, augmented by a driving, often funky attack.

Hip—knowledgeable.

Loot—money.

Progressive jazz—term used by Stan Kenton to describe music played by his orchestra on a concert tour in 1947; since then sometimes applied generically to postwar jazz.

Rhythm section—in postwar jazz groups, usually piano, bass and drums; guitar is added by some groups playing in prewar swing style.

Session—recording performance.

Sit in—to join a musical group for a few selections.

Soul jazz—jazz based on the mannerisms of gospel music.

Sweet music—melodic dance music with no strong relationship to jazz.

Swing era—the late 1930's and early 1940's when the big swing bands (Benny Goodman, Artie Shaw, Harry James) were at the height of their popularity.

Third stream—music which is neither "classical" nor jazz but draws on elements of both.

Up-tempo—a fast tempo.

West Coast jazz—an extension of cool jazz as played by various groups in California during the early 1950's.

Discography

CHAPTER TWO

Lester Young, "Memorial Album," Epic SN 6031.

Lester Young, "With the Kansas City Six," Mainstream 56012, stereo 6012.

Charlie Christian, "With the Benny Goodman Sextet," Columbia CL 652.

Dizzy Gillespie-Charlie Christian, "1941," Counterpoint 548.

Charlie Parker, "The Genius of Charlie Parker," Savoy 12009, 12014.

CHAPTER THREE

Miles Davis, "Birth of the Cool," Capitol T 1974.

Miles Davis, "Miles Ahead," Columbia CL 1041, stereo CS 8633.

Stan Getz, "Greatest Hits," Prestige 7337.

Lennie Tristano, "The New Tristano," Atlantic 1357.

Lee Konitz, "Subconscious-Lee," Prestige 7250.

Shorty Rogers, "Modern Sounds," Capitol T 2025, stereo DT 2025.

Gerry Mulligan, "California Concerts," Pacific Jazz 50.

CHAPTER FOUR

Horace Silver, "Six Pieces of Silver," Blue Note 1539.

Jimmy Giuffre, "Trav'lin' Light," Atlantic 1254.

Ray Charles, "Live in Concert," ABC-Paramount 500, stereo S–500.

Sonny Rollins, "Contemporary Leaders," Contemporary 3564, stereo 7564.

John Coltrane, "My Favorite Things," Atlantic 1361, stereo S 1361.

Ornette Coleman, "This Is Our Music," Atlantic 1353, stereo S 1353.

Thelonious Monk, "Monk," Columbia CL 2291, stereo CS 9091.

Charlie Mingus, "The Black Saint," Impulse 35, stereo S 35.

CHAPTER FIVE

Stan Kenton, "Artistry in Rhythm," Capitol T 167.

Dave Brubeck, "Time Out," Columbia CL 1397, stereo CS 8192.

Modern Jazz Quartet, "European Concert," Atlantic 2–603, stereo S2–603.

Gunther Schuller, Atlantic 1365, stereo S–1365.

George Russell, "Jazz in the Space Age," Decca 9219, stereo 79219.

"Outstanding Jazz Compositions of the 20th Century," Columbia C2L 31, stereo C2S 831.

CHAPTER SIX

Bunk Johnson, Good Time Jazz 12048.

George Lewis, "Concert," Blue Note 1208.

Kid Ory, "Favorites," Good Time Jazz 12041/2, stereo 10041/2.

Lu Watters, "San Francisco Style," Good Time Jazz 12001/3.

Turk Murphy, "San Francisco Jazz," Good Time Jazz 12026/7.

Dukes of Dixieland, "Best," Audio Fidelity 1962, stereo 5962.

Woody Herman, "The Thundering Herds," Columbia C3L 25.

Bibliography

Balliett, Whitney, *Dinosaurs in the Morning*. Philadelphia, J. B. Lippincott Co., 1962.

——, *The Sound of Surprise*. New York, E. P. Dutton & Co., 1959.

Feather, Leonard, *The Book of Jazz*. New York, Horizon Press, 1965.

Goldberg, Joe, *Jazz Masters of the '50s*. New York, The Macmillan Co., 1965.

Harrison, Max, *Charlie Parker*. New York, A. S. Barnes & Co., 1961.

Hentoff, Nat, *The Jazz Life*. New York, Dial Press, 1961.

Hodeir, André, *Jazz: Its Evolution and Essence*. New York, Grove Press, 1961.

James, Michael, *Dizzy Gillespie*. New York, A. S. Barnes & Co., 1961.

——, *Miles Davis*. New York, A. S. Barnes & Co., 1961.

Reisner, Robert George, *Bird: The Legend of Charlie Parker*. New York, Citadel Press, 1962.

INDEX